Drive

Drive

THE SURPRISING TRUTH

ABOUT WHAT MOTIVATES US

Daniel H. Pink

RIVERHEAD BOOKS

a member of Penguin Group (USA) Inc.

New York

2009

RIVERHEAD BOOKS
Published by the Penguin Group
Penguin Group (USA) Inc., 375 Hudson Street, New York, New York 10014, USA •
Penguin Group (Canada), 90 Eglinton Avenue East, Suite 700, Toronto, Ontario
M4P 2Y3, Canada (a division of Pearson Penguin Canada Inc.) • Penguin Books Ltd,
80 Strand, London WC2R 0RL, England • Penguin Ireland, 25 St Stephen's Green,
Dublin 2, Ireland (a division of Penguin Books Ltd) • Penguin Group (Australia),
250 Camberwell Road, Camberwell, Victoria 3124, Australia (a division of Pearson
Australia Group Pty Ltd) • Penguin Books India Pvt Ltd, 11 Community Centre,
Panchsheel Park, New Delhi–110 017, India • Penguin Group (NZ), 67 Apollo
Drive, Rosedale, North Shore 0632, New Zealand (a division of Pearson
New Zealand Ltd) • Penguin Books (South Africa) (Pty) Ltd, 24 Sturdee
Avenue, Rosebank, Johannesburg 2196, South Africa

Penguin Books Ltd, Registered Offices: 80 Strand, London WC2R 0RL, England

Library of Congress Cataloging-in-Publication Data
Pink, Daniel H.
Drive : the surprising truth about what motivates us / Daniel H. Pink.
p.   cm.
Includes bibliographical references and index.
ISBN 978-1-59448-884-9
1. Motivation (Psychology).   I. Title.
BF503.P475   2009   2009040651
153.1'534—dc22

Printed in the United States of America
15   17   19   20   18   16   14

BOOK DESIGN BY AMANDA DEWEY

For Sophia, Eliza, and Saul—

the surprising trio that motivates me

CONTENTS

> *"In scientific terms, it was akin to rolling a steel ball down an inclined plane to measure its velocity—only to watch the ball float into the air instead. It suggested that our understanding of the gravitational pulls on our behavior was inadequate— that what we thought were fixed laws had plenty of loopholes."*

Part One

A New Operating System

> *"But in the first ten years of this century—a period of truly staggering underachievement in business, technology, and social progress—we've*

*discovered that this sturdy, old operating system doesn't work nearly
as well. It crashes—often and unpredictably. It forces people to devise
workarounds to bypass its flaws. Most of all, it is proving incompatible
with many aspects of contemporary business."*

CHAPTER 2. Seven Reasons Carrots and Sticks (Often) Don't Work . . .

*"In other words, rewards can perform a weird sort of behavioral alchemy:
They can transform an interesting task into a drudge. They can turn play
into work."*

CHAPTER 2A. . . . and the Special Circumstances When They Do

*"While an operating system centered around rewards and punishments has
outlived its usefulness and badly needs an upgrade, that doesn't mean we
should scrap its every piece."*

CHAPTER 3. Type I and Type X

*"A picture may be worth a thousand words—but sometimes neither is as
potent as just two letters."*

Part Two

The Three Elements

CHAPTER 4. Autonomy

"Perhaps it's time to toss the very word 'management' into the linguistic ash heap alongside 'icebox' and 'horseless carriage.' This era doesn't call for better management. It calls for a renaissance of self-direction."

CHAPTER 5. Mastery

"In our offices and our classrooms we have way too much compliance and way too little engagement. The former might get you through the day, but only the latter will get you through the night."

CHAPTER 6. Purpose

"It's in our nature to seek purpose. But that nature is now being revealed and expressed on a scale that is demographically unprecedented and, until recently, scarcely imaginable. The consequences could rejuvenate our businesses and remake our world."

Part Three

The Type I Toolkit

Drive

The Puzzling Puzzles of
Harry Harlow and Edward Deci

In the middle of the last century, two young scientists conducted experiments that should have changed the world—but did not.

Harry F. Harlow was a professor of psychology at the University of Wisconsin who, in the 1940s, established one of the world's first laboratories for studying primate behavior. One day in 1949, Harlow and two colleagues gathered eight rhesus monkeys for a two-week experiment on learning. The researchers devised a simple mechanical puzzle like the one pictured on the next page. Solving it required three steps: pull out the vertical pin, undo the hook, and lift the hinged cover. Pretty easy for you and me, far more challenging for a thirteen-pound lab monkey.

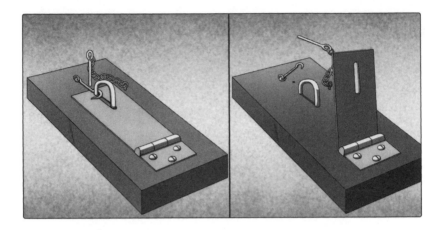

Harlow's puzzle in the starting (left) and solved (right) positions.

The experimenters placed the puzzles in the monkeys' cages to observe how they reacted—and to prepare them for tests of their problem-solving prowess at the end of the two weeks. But almost immediately, something strange happened. Unbidden by any outside urging and unprompted by the experimenters, the monkeys began playing with the puzzles with focus, determination, and what looked like enjoyment. And in short order, they began figuring out how the contraptions worked. By the time Harlow tested the monkeys on days 13 and 14 of the experiment, the primates had become quite adept. They solved the puzzles frequently and quickly; two-thirds of the time they cracked the code in less than sixty seconds.

Now, this was a bit odd. Nobody had taught the monkeys how to remove the pin, slide the hook, and open the cover. Nobody had rewarded them with food, affection, or even quiet applause when they succeeded. And that ran counter to the accepted notions of how primates—including the bigger-brained, less hairy primates known as human beings—behaved.

Scientists then knew that two main drives powered behavior. The first was the biological drive. Humans and other animals ate to sate their hunger, drank to quench their thirst, and copulated to satisfy their carnal urges. But that wasn't happening here. "Solution did not lead to food, water, or sex gratification," Harlow reported.[1]

But the only other known drive also failed to explain the monkeys' peculiar behavior. If biological motivations came from within, this second drive came from without—the rewards and punishments the environment delivered for behaving in certain ways. This was certainly true for humans, who responded exquisitely to such external forces. If you promised to raise our pay, we'd work harder. If you held out the prospect of getting an A on the test, we'd study longer. If you threatened to dock us for showing up late or for incorrectly completing a form, we'd arrive on time and tick every box. But that didn't account for the monkeys' actions either. As Harlow wrote, and you can almost hear him scratching his head, "The behavior obtained in this investigation poses some interesting questions for motivation theory, since significant learning was attained and efficient performance maintained without resort to special or extrinsic incentives."

What else could it be?

To answer the question, Harlow offered a novel theory—what amounted to a *third* drive: "The performance of the task," he said, "provided intrinsic reward." The monkeys solved the puzzles simply because they found it gratifying to solve puzzles. They enjoyed it. The joy of the task was its own reward.

If this notion was radical, what happened next only deepened the confusion and controversy. Perhaps this newly discovered drive— Harlow eventually called it "intrinsic motivation"—was real. But surely it was subordinate to the other two drives. If the monkeys were rewarded—with raisins!—for solving the puzzles, they'd no doubt perform even better. Yet when Harlow tested that approach, the monkeys actually made *more* errors and solved the puzzles *less* frequently. "Introduction of food in the present experiment," Harlow wrote, "served to disrupt performance, a phenomenon not reported in the literature."

Now, this was *really* odd. In scientific terms, it was akin to rolling a steel ball down an inclined plane to measure its velocity—only to watch the ball float into the air instead. It suggested that our understanding of the gravitational pulls on our behavior was inadequate—that what we thought were fixed laws had plenty of loopholes. Harlow emphasized the "strength and persistence" of the monkeys' drive to complete the puzzles. Then he noted:

> It would appear that this drive . . . may be as basic and strong as the [other] drives. Furthermore, there is some reason to believe that [it] can be as efficient in facilitating learning.[2]

At the time, however, the prevailing two drives held a tight grip on scientific thinking. So Harlow sounded the alarm. He urged scientists to "close down large sections of our theoretical junkyard" and offer fresher, more accurate accounts of human behavior.[3] He warned that our explanation of why we did what we did was incomplete. He said that to truly understand the human condition, we had to take account of this third drive.

Then he pretty much dropped the whole idea.

Rather than battle the establishment and begin offering a more complete view of motivation, Harlow abandoned this contentious line of research and later became famous for studies on the science of affection.[4] His notion of this third drive bounced around the psychological literature, but it remained on the periphery—of behavioral science and of our understanding of ourselves. It would be two decades before another scientist picked up the thread that Harlow had so provocatively left on that Wisconsin laboratory table.

In the summer of 1969, Edward Deci was a Carnegie Mellon University psychology graduate student in search of a dissertation topic. Deci, who had already earned an MBA from Wharton, was intrigued by motivation but suspected that scholars and businesspeople had misunderstood it. So, tearing a page from the Harlow playbook, he set out to study the topic with the help of a puzzle.

Deci chose the Soma puzzle cube, a then popular Parker Brothers offering that, thanks to YouTube, retains something of a cult following today. The puzzle, shown below, consists of seven plastic pieces—six comprising four one-inch cubes, one comprising three one-inch cubes. Players can assemble the seven pieces into a few million possible combinations—from abstract shapes to recognizable objects.

The seven pieces of the Soma puzzle unassembled (left) and then fashioned into one of several million possible configurations.

For the study, Deci divided participants, male and female university students, into an experimental group (what I'll call Group A) and a control group (what I'll call Group B). Each participated in three one-hour sessions held on consecutive days.

Here's how the sessions worked: Each participant entered a room and sat at a table on top of which were the seven Soma puzzle pieces, drawings of three puzzle configurations, and copies of *Time, The New Yorker*, and *Playboy*. (Hey, it was 1969.) Deci sat on the opposite end of the table to explain the instructions and to time performance with a stopwatch.

In the first session, members of both groups had to assemble the Soma pieces to replicate the configurations before them. In the second session, they did the same thing with different drawings—only this time Deci told Group A that they'd be paid $1 (the equivalent of nearly $6 today) for every configuration they successfully reproduced. Group B, meanwhile, got new drawings but no pay. Finally, in the third session, both groups received new drawings and had to reproduce them for no compensation, just as in session one. (See the table below.)

HOW THE TWO GROUPS WERE TREATED

	Day 1	Day 2	Day 3
Group A	*No reward*	*Reward*	*No reward*
Group B	*No reward*	*No reward*	*No reward*

The twist came midway through each session. After a participant had assembled the Soma puzzle pieces to match two of the three drawings, Deci halted the proceedings. He said that he was going to give them a fourth drawing—but to choose the right one, he needed to feed their completion times into a computer. And—this being the late 1960s, when room-straddling mainframes were the norm and desktop PCs were still a decade away—that meant he had to leave for a little while.

On the way out, he said, "I shall be gone only a few minutes, you may do whatever you like while I'm gone." But Deci wasn't really plugging numbers into an ancient teletype. Instead, he walked to an adjoining room connected to the experiment room by a one-way window. Then, for exactly eight minutes, he watched what people did when left alone. Did they continue fiddling with the puzzle, perhaps attempting to reproduce the third drawing? Or did they do something else—page through the magazines, check out the center-fold, stare into space, catch a quick nap?

In the first session, not surprisingly, there wasn't much difference between what the Group A and Group B participants did during that secretly watched eight-minute free-choice period. Both continued playing with the puzzle, on average, for between three and a half and four minutes, suggesting they found it at least somewhat interesting.

On the second day, during which Group A participants were paid for each successful configuration and Group B participants were not, the unpaid group behaved mostly as they had during the first free-choice period. But the paid group suddenly got *really* interested in Soma puzzles. On average, the people in Group A spent more than five minutes messing with the puzzle, perhaps getting a head start on that third challenge or gearing up for the chance to earn some beer money when Deci returned. This makes intuitive sense, right? It's consistent with what we believe about motivation: Reward me and I'll work harder.

Yet what happened on the third day confirmed Deci's own suspicions about the peculiar workings of motivation—and gently called into question a guiding premise of modern life. This time, Deci told the participants in Group A that there was only enough money to pay them for one day and that this third session would therefore be unpaid. Then things unfolded just as before—two puzzles, followed by Deci's interruption.

During the ensuing eight-minute free-choice period, the subjects in the never-been-paid Group B actually played with the puzzle for a little longer than they had in previous sessions. Maybe they were becoming ever more engaged; maybe it was just a statistical quirk. But the subjects in Group A, who previously had been paid, responded differently. They now spent significantly *less* time playing with the puzzle—not only about two minutes less than during their paid session, but about a full minute less than in the first session when they initially encountered, and obviously enjoyed, the puzzles.

In an echo of what Harlow discovered two decades earlier, Deci revealed that human motivation seemed to operate by laws that ran counter to what most scientists and citizens believed. From the office to the playing field, we knew what got people going. Rewards—especially cold, hard cash—intensified interest and enhanced performance. What Deci found, and then confirmed in two additional studies he conducted shortly thereafter, was almost the opposite. "When money is used as an external reward for some activity, the subjects lose intrinsic interest for the activity," he wrote.[5] Rewards can deliver a short-term boost—just as a jolt of caffeine can keep you cranking for a few more hours. But the effect wears off—and, worse, can reduce a person's longer-term motivation to continue the project.

Human beings, Deci said, have an "inherent tendency to seek out novelty and challenges, to extend and exercise their capacities, to explore, and to learn." But this third drive was more fragile than the other two; it needed the right environment to survive. "One who is interested in developing and enhancing intrinsic motivation in children, employees, students, etc., should not concentrate on external-control systems such as monetary rewards," he wrote in a follow-up paper.[6] Thus began what for Deci became a lifelong quest to rethink why we do what we do—a pursuit that sometimes put him at odds with fellow psychologists, got him fired from a business school, and challenged the operating assumptions of organizations everywhere.

"It was controversial," Deci told me one spring morning forty years after the Soma experiments. "Nobody was expecting rewards would have a negative effect."

THIS IS A BOOK about motivation. I will show that much of what we believe about the subject just isn't so—and that the insights that Harlow and Deci began uncovering a few decades ago come much closer to the truth. The problem is that most businesses haven't caught up to this new understanding of what motivates us. Too many organizations—not just companies, but governments and nonprofits as well—still operate from assumptions about human potential and individual performance that are outdated, unexamined, and rooted more in folklore than in science. They continue to pursue practices such as short-term incentive plans and pay-for-performance schemes in the face of mounting evidence that such measures usually don't work and often do harm. Worse, these practices have infiltrated our schools, where we ply our future workforce with iPods, cash, and pizza coupons to "incentivize" them to learn. Something has gone wrong.

The good news is that the solution stands before us—in the work of a band of behavioral scientists who have carried on the pioneering efforts of Harlow and Deci and whose quiet work over the last half-century offers us a more dynamic view of human motivation. For too long, there's been a mismatch between what science knows and what business does. The goal of this book is to repair that breach.

Drive has three parts. Part One will look at the flaws in our reward-and-punishment system and propose a new way to think about motivation. Chapter 1 will examine how the prevailing view of motivation is becoming incompatible with many aspects of contemporary business and life. Chapter 2 will reveal the seven reasons why carrot-and-stick extrinsic motivators often produce the opposite of what they set out to achieve. (Following that is a short addendum, Chapter 2a, that shows the special circumstances when carrots and sticks actually can be effective.) Chapter 3 will introduce what I call "Type I" behavior, a way of thinking and an approach to business grounded in the real science of human motivation and powered by our third drive—our innate need to direct our own lives, to learn and create new things, and to do better by ourselves and our world.

Part Two will examine the three elements of Type I behavior and show how individuals and organizations are using them to improve performance and deepen satisfaction. Chapter 4 will explore autonomy, our desire to be self-directed. Chapter 5 will look at mastery, our urge to get better and better at what we do. Chapter 6 will explore purpose, our yearning to be part of something larger than ourselves.

Part Three, the Type I Toolkit, is a comprehensive set of resources to help you create settings in which Type I behavior can flourish. Here you'll find everything from dozens of exercises to awaken motivation in yourself and others, to discussion questions for your book club, to a supershort summary of *Drive* that will help you fake your way through a cocktail party. And while this book is mostly about business, in this section I'll offer some thoughts about how to apply these concepts to education and to our lives outside of work.

But before we get down to all that, let's begin with a thought experiment, one that requires going back in time—to the days when John Major was Britain's prime minister, Barack Obama was a skinny young law professor, Internet connections were dial-up, and a black-berry was still just a fruit.

Part One

A New
Operating System

CHAPTER 1

The Rise and Fall
of Motivation 2.0

Imagine it's 1995. You sit down with an economist—an accomplished business school professor with a Ph.D. in economics. You say to her: "I've got a crystal ball here that can peer fifteen years into the future. I'd like to test your forecasting powers."

She's skeptical, but she decides to humor you.

"I'm going to describe two new encyclopedias—one just out, the other to be launched in a few years. You have to predict which will be more successful in 2010."

"Bring it," she says.

"The first encyclopedia comes from Microsoft. As you know, Microsoft is already a large and profitable company. And with this year's introduction of Windows 95, it's about to become an era-defining colossus. Microsoft will fund this encyclopedia. It will pay professional writers and editors to craft articles on thousands of topics. Well-compensated managers will oversee the project to ensure it's completed on budget and on time. Then Microsoft will sell the encyclopedia on CD-ROMs and later online.

"The second encyclopedia won't come from a company. It will be created by tens of thousands of people who write and edit articles for fun. These hobbyists won't need any special qualifications to participate. And nobody will be paid a dollar or a euro or a yen to write or edit articles. Participants will have to contribute their labor—sometimes twenty and thirty hours per week—for free. The encyclopedia itself, which will exist online, will also be free—no charge for anyone who wants to use it.

"Now," you say to the economist, "think forward fifteen years. According to my crystal ball, in 2010, one of these encyclopedias will be the largest and most popular in the world and the other will be defunct. Which is which?"

In 1995, I doubt you could have a found a single sober economist anywhere on planet Earth who would not have picked that first model as the success. Any other conclusion would have been laughable—contrary to nearly every business principle she taught her students. It would have been like asking a zoologist who would win a 200-meter footrace between a cheetah and your brother-in-law. Not even close.

Sure, that ragtag band of volunteers might produce something. But there was no way its product could compete with an offering from a powerful profit-driven company. The incentives were all wrong. Microsoft stood to gain from the success of its product; everyone involved in the other project knew from the outset that success would earn them nothing. Most important, Microsoft's writers, editors, and managers were paid. The other project's contributors were not. In fact, it probably *cost* them money each time they performed free work instead of remunerative labor. The question was such a no-brainer that our economist wouldn't even have considered putting it on an exam for her MBA class. It was too easy.

But you know how things turned out.

On October 31, 2009, Microsoft pulled the plug on *MSN Encarta*, its disc and online encyclopedia, which had been on the market for sixteen years. Meanwhile, Wikipedia—that second model—ended up becoming the largest and most popular encyclopedia in the world. Just eight years after its inception, Wikipedia had more than 13 million articles in some 260 languages, including 3 million in English alone.[1]

What happened? The conventional view of human motivation has a very hard time explaining this result.

THE TRIUMPH OF CARROTS AND STICKS

Computers—whether the giant mainframes in Deci's experiments, the iMac on which I'm writing this sentence, or the mobile phone chirping in your pocket— all have operating systems. Beneath the surface of the hardware you touch and the programs you manipulate is a complex layer of software that contains the instructions, protocols, and suppositions that enable everything to function smoothly. Most of us don't think much about operating systems. We notice them only when they start failing—when the hardware and software they're supposed to manage grow too large and complicated for the current operating system to handle. Then our computer starts crashing. We complain. And smart software developers, who've always been tinkering with pieces of the program, sit down to write a fundamentally better one—an upgrade.

Societies also have operating systems. The laws, social customs, and economic arrangements that we encounter each day sit atop a layer of instructions, protocols, and suppositions about how the world works. And much of our societal operating system consists of a set of assumptions about human behavior.

In our very early days—I mean *very* early days, say, fifty thousand years ago—the underlying assumption about human behavior was simple and true. We were trying to survive. From roaming the savannah to gather food to scrambling for the bushes when a saber-toothed tiger approached, that drive guided most of our behavior. Call this early operating system Motivation 1.0. It wasn't especially elegant, nor was it much different from those of rhesus monkeys, giant apes, or many other animals. But it served us nicely. It worked well. Until it didn't.

As humans formed more complex societies, bumping up against strangers and needing to cooperate in order to get things done, an operating system based purely on the biological drive was inadequate. In fact, sometimes we needed ways to *restrain* this drive—to prevent me from swiping your dinner and you from stealing my spouse. And so in a feat of remarkable cultural engineering, we slowly replaced what we had with a version more compatible with how we'd begun working and living.

At the core of this new and improved operating system was a revised and more accurate assumption: Humans are more than the sum of our biological urges. That first drive still mattered—no doubt about that—but it didn't fully account for who we are. We also had a second drive—to seek reward and avoid punishment more broadly. And it was from this insight that a new operating system— call it Motivation 2.0—arose. (Of course, other animals also respond to rewards and punishments, but only humans have proved able to channel this drive to develop everything from contract law to convenience stores.)

Harnessing this second drive has been essential to economic progress around the world, especially during the last two centuries. Consider the Industrial Revolution. Technological developments—steam engines, railroads, widespread electricity—played a crucial role in fostering the growth of industry. But so did less tangible innovations—in particular, the work of an American engineer named Frederick Winslow Taylor. In the early 1900s, Taylor, who believed businesses were being run in an inefficient, haphazard way, invented what he called "scientific management." His invention was a form of "software" expertly crafted to run atop the Motivation 2.0 platform. And it was widely and quickly adopted.

Workers, this approach held, were like parts in a complicated machine. If they did the right work in the right way at the right time, the machine would function smoothly. And to ensure that happened, you simply rewarded the behavior you sought and punished the behavior you discouraged. People would respond rationally to these external forces—these extrinsic motivators—and both they and the system itself would flourish. We tend to think that coal and oil have powered economic development. But in some sense, the engine of commerce has been fueled equally by carrots and sticks.

The Motivation 2.0 operating system has endured for a very long time. Indeed, it is so deeply embedded in our lives that most of us scarcely recognize that it exists. For as long as any of us can remember, we've configured our organizations and constructed our lives around its bedrock assumption: The way to improve performance, increase productivity, and encourage excellence is to reward the good and punish the bad.

Despite its greater sophistication and higher aspirations, Motivation 2.0 still wasn't exactly ennobling. It suggested that, in the end, human beings aren't much different from horses—that the way to get us moving in the right direction is by dangling a crunchier carrot or wielding a sharper stick. But what this operating system lacked in enlightenment, it made up for in effectiveness. It worked well—extremely well. Until it didn't.

As the twentieth century progressed, as economies grew still more complex, and as the people in them had to deploy new, more sophisticated skills, the Motivation 2.0 approach encountered some resistance. In the 1950s, Abraham Maslow, a former student of Harry Harlow's at the University of Wisconsin, developed the field of humanistic psychology, which questioned the idea that human behavior was purely the ratlike seeking of positive stimuli and avoidance of negative stimuli. In 1960, MIT management professor Douglas McGregor imported some of Maslow's ideas to the business world. McGregor challenged the presumption that humans are fundamentally inert—that absent external rewards and punishments, we wouldn't do much. People have other, higher drives, he said. And these drives could benefit businesses if managers and business leaders respected them. Thanks in part to McGregor's writing, companies evolved a bit. Dress codes relaxed, schedules became more flexible. Many organizations looked for ways to grant employees greater autonomy and to help them grow. These refinements repaired some weaknesses, but they amounted to a modest improvement rather than a thorough upgrade—Motivation 2.1.

And so this general approach remained intact—because it was, after all, easy to understand, simple to monitor, and straightforward to enforce. But in the first ten years of this century—a period of truly staggering underachievement in business, technology, and social progress—we've discovered that this sturdy, old operating system doesn't work nearly as well. It crashes—often and unpredictably. It forces people to devise workarounds to bypass its flaws. Most of all, it is proving incompatible with many aspects of contemporary business. And if we examine those incompatibility problems closely, we'll realize that modest updates—a patch here or there—will not solve the problem. What we need is a full-scale upgrade.

THREE INCOMPATIBILITY PROBLEMS

Motivation 2.0 still serves some purposes well. It's just deeply unreliable. Sometimes it works; many times it doesn't. And understanding its defects will help determine which parts to keep and which to discard as we fashion an upgrade. The glitches fall into three broad categories. Our current operating system has become far less compatible with, and at times downright antagonistic to: how we *organize* what we do; how we *think about* what we do; and how we *do* what we do.

How We Organize What We Do

Go back to that encyclopedic showdown between Microsoft and Wikipedia. The assumptions at the heart of Motivation 2.0 suggest that such a result shouldn't even be possible. Wikipedia's triumph seems to defy the laws of behavioral physics.

Now, if this all-volunteer, all-amateur encyclopedia were the only instance of its kind, we might dismiss it as an aberration, an exception that proves the rule. But it's not. Instead, Wikipedia represents the most powerful new business model of the twenty-first century: open source.

Fire up your home computer, for example. When you visit the Web to check the weather forecast or order some sneakers, you might be using Firefox, a free open-source Web browser created almost exclusively by volunteers around the world. Unpaid laborers who give away their product? That couldn't be sustainable. The incentives are all wrong. Yet Firefox now has more than 150 million users.

Or walk into the IT department of a large company anywhere in the world and ask for a tour. That company's corporate computer servers could well run on Linux, software devised by an army of unpaid programmers and available for free. Linux now powers one in four corporate servers. Then ask an employee to explain how the company's website works. Humming beneath the site is probably Apache, free open-source Web server software created and maintained by a far-flung global group of volunteers. Apache's share of the corporate Web server market: 52 percent. In other words, companies that typically rely on external rewards to manage their employees run some of their most important systems with products created by nonemployees who don't seem to need such rewards.

And it's not just the tens of thousands of software projects across the globe. Today you can find: open-source cookbooks; open-source textbooks; open-source car design; open-source medical research; open-source legal briefs; open-source stock photography; open-source prosthetics; open-source credit unions; open-source cola; and for those for whom soft drinks won't suffice, open-source beer.

This new way of organizing what we do doesn't banish extrinsic rewards. People in the open-source movement haven't taken vows of poverty. For many, participation in these projects can burnish their reputations and sharpen their skills, which can enhance their earning power. Entrepreneurs have launched new, and sometimes lucrative, companies to help organizations implement and maintain open-source software applications.

But ultimately, open source depends on intrinsic motivation with the same ferocity that older business models rely on extrinsic motivation, as several scholars have shown. MIT management professor Karim Lakhani and Boston Consulting Group consultant Bob Wolf surveyed 684 open-source developers, mostly in North America and Europe, about why they participated in these projects. Lakhani and Wolf uncovered a range of motives, but they found "that enjoyment-based intrinsic motivation, namely how creative a person feels when working on the project, is the strongest and most pervasive driver."[2] A large majority of programmers, the researchers discovered, reported that they frequently reached the state of optimal challenge called "flow." Likewise, three German economists who studied open-source projects around the world found that what drives participants is "a set of predominantly intrinsic motives"—in particular, "the fun . . . of mastering the challenge of a given software problem" and the "desire to give a gift to the programmer community."[3] Motivation 2.0 has little room for these sorts of impulses.

What's more, open source is only one way people are restructuring what they do along new organizational lines and atop different motivational ground. Let's move from software code to the legal code. The laws in most developed countries permit essentially two types of business organizations—profit and nonprofit. One makes money, the other does good. And the most prominent member of that first category is the publicly held corporation—owned by shareholders and run by managers who are overseen by a board of directors. The managers and directors bear one overriding responsibility: to maximize shareholder gain. Other types of business organizations steer by the same rules of the road. In the United States, for instance, partnerships, S corporations, C corporations, limited liability corporations, and other business configurations all aim toward a common end. The objective of those who run them—practically, legally, in some ways morally—is to maximize profit.

Let me give a rousing, heartfelt, and grateful cheer for these business forms and the farsighted countries that enable their citizens to create them. Without them, our lives would be infinitely less prosperous, less healthy, and less happy. But in the last few years, several people around the world have been changing the recipe and cooking up new varieties of business organizations.

For example, in April 2008, Vermont became the first U.S. state to allow a new type of business called the "low-profit limited liability corporation." Dubbed an L3C, this entity is a corporation—but not as we typically think of it. As one report explained, an L3C "operate[s] like a for-profit business generating at least modest profits, but its primary aim [is] to offer significant social benefits." Three other U.S. states have followed Vermont's lead.[4] An L3C in North Carolina, for instance, is buying abandoned furniture factories in the state, updating them with green technology, and leasing them back to beleaguered furniture manufacturers at a low rate. The venture hopes to make money, but its real purpose is to help revitalize a struggling region.

Meanwhile, Nobel Peace Prize winner Muhammad Yunus has begun creating what he calls "social businesses." These are companies that raise capital, develop products, and sell them in an open market but do so in the service of a larger social mission—or as he puts it, "with the profit-maximization principle replaced by the social-benefit principle." The Fourth Sector Network in the United States and Denmark is promoting "the for-benefit organization"—a hybrid that it says represents a new category of organization that is both economically self-sustaining and animated by a public purpose. One example: Mozilla, the entity that gave us Firefox, is organized as a "for-benefit" organization. And three U.S. entrepreneurs have invented the "B Corporation," a designation that requires companies to amend their bylaws so that the incentives favor long-term value and social impact instead of short-term economic gain.[5]

Neither open-source production nor previously unimagined "not only for profit" businesses are yet the norm, of course. And they won't consign the public corporation to the trash heap. But their emergence tells us something important about where we're heading. "There's a big movement out there that is not yet recognized as a movement," a lawyer who specializes in for-benefit organizations told *The New York Times*.[6] One reason could be that traditional businesses are profit maximizers, which square perfectly with Motivation 2.0. These new entities are *purpose maximizers*—which are unsuited to this older operating system because they flout its very principles.

How We Think About What We Do

When I took my first economics course back in the early 1980s, our professor—a brilliant lecturer with a Patton-like stage presence—offered an important clarification before she'd chalked her first indifference curve on the blackboard. Economics, she explained, wasn't the study of money. It was the study of behavior. In the course of a day, each of us was constantly figuring the cost and benefits of our actions and then deciding how to act. Economists studied what people did, rather than what we said, because we did what was best for us. We were rational calculators of our economic self-interest.

When I studied law a few years later, a similar idea reappeared. The newly ascendant field of "law and economics" held that precisely because we were such awesome self-interest calculators, laws and regulations often impeded, rather than permitted, sensible and just outcomes. I survived law school in no small part because I discovered the talismanic phrase and offered it on exams: "In a world of perfect information and low transaction costs, the parties will bargain to a wealth-maximizing result."

Then, about a decade later, came a curious turn of events that made me question much of what I'd worked hard, and taken on enormous debt, to learn. In 2002, the Nobel Foundation awarded its prize in economics to a guy who wasn't even an economist. And they gave him the field's highest honor largely for revealing that we *weren't* always rational calculators of our economic self-interest and that the parties often *didn't* bargain to a wealth-maximizing result. Daniel Kahneman, an American psychologist who won the Nobel Prize in economics that year for work he'd done with Israeli Amos Tversky, helped force a change in how we think about what we do. And one of the implications of this new way of thinking is that it calls into question many of the assumptions of Motivation 2.0.

Kahneman and others in the field of behavioral economics agreed with my professor that economics was the study of human economic behavior. They just believed that we'd placed too much emphasis on the *economic* and not enough on the *human*. That hyperrational calculator-brained person wasn't real. He was a convenient fiction.

Play a game with me and I'll try to illustrate the point. Suppose somebody gives me ten dollars and tells me to share it—some, all, or none—with you. If you accept my offer, we both get to keep the money. If you reject it, neither of us gets anything. If I offered you six dollars (keeping four for myself), would you take it? Almost certainly. If I offered you five, you'd probably take that, too. But what if I offered you two dollars? Would you take it? In an experiment replicated around the world, most people rejected offers of two dollars and below.[7] That makes no sense in terms of wealth maximization. If you take my offer of two dollars, you're two dollars richer. If you reject it, you get nothing. Your cognitive calculator knows two is greater than zero—but because you're a human being, your notions of fair play or your desire for revenge or your simple irritation overrides it.

In real life our behavior is far more complex than the textbook allows and often confounds the idea that we're purely rational. We don't save enough for retirement even though it's to our clear economic advantage to do so. We hang on to bad investments longer than we should, because we feel far sharper pain from losing money than we do from gaining the exact same amount. Give us a choice of two television sets, we'll pick one; toss in an irrelevant third choice, and we'll pick the other. In short, we are irrational—and predictably so, says economist Dan Ariely, author of *Predictably Irrational*, a book that offers an entertaining and engaging overview of behavioral economics.

The trouble for our purposes is that Motivation 2.0 assumes we're the same robotic wealth-maximizers I was taught we were a couple of decades ago. Indeed, the very premise of extrinsic incentives is that we'll always respond rationally to them. But even most economists don't believe that anymore. Sometimes these motivators work. Often they don't. And many times, they inflict collateral damage. In short, the new way economists think about what we do is hard to reconcile with Motivation 2.0.

What's more, if people do things for lunk-headed, backward-looking reasons, why wouldn't we also do things for significance-seeking, self-actualizing reasons? If we're predictably irrational—and we clearly are—why couldn't we also be predictably transcendent?

If that seems far-fetched, consider some of our other bizarre behaviors. We leave lucrative jobs to take low-paying ones that provide a clearer sense of purpose. We work to master the clarinet on weekends although we have little hope of making a dime (Motivation 2.0) or acquiring a mate (Motivation 1.0) from doing so. We play with puzzles even when we don't get a few raisins or dollars for solving them.

Some scholars are already widening the reach of behavioral economics to encompass these ideas. The most prominent is Bruno Frey, an economist at the University of Zurich. Like the behavioral economists, he has argued that we need to move beyond the idea of *Homo Oeconomicus* (Economic Man, that fictional wealth-maximizing robot). But his extension goes in a slightly different direction—to what he calls *Homo Oeconomicus Maturus* (or Mature Economic Man). This figure, he says, "is more 'mature' in the sense that he is endowed with a more refined motivational structure." In other words, to fully understand human economic behavior, we have to come to terms with an idea at odds with Motivation 2.0. As Frey writes, "Intrinsic motivation is of *great importance* for all economic activities. It is inconceivable that people are motivated solely or even mainly by external incentives."[8]

How We Do What We Do

If you manage other people, take a quick glance over your shoulder. There's a ghost hovering there. His name is Frederick Winslow Taylor—remember him from earlier in the chapter?—and he's whispering in your ear. "Work," Taylor is murmuring, "consists mainly of simple, not particularly interesting, tasks. The only way to get people to do them is to incentivize them properly and monitor them carefully." In the early 1900s, Taylor had a point. Today, in much of the world, that's less true. Yes, for some people work remains routine, unchallenging, and directed by others. But for a surprisingly large number of people, jobs have become more complex, more interesting, and more self-directed. And that type of work presents a direct challenge to the assumptions of Motivation 2.0.

Begin with complexity. Behavioral scientists often divide what we do on the job or learn in school into two categories: "algorithmic" and "heuristic." An algorithmic task is one in which you follow a set of established instructions down a single pathway to one conclusion. That is, there's an algorithm for solving it. A heuristic task is the opposite. Precisely because no algorithm exists for it, you have to experiment with possibilities and devise a novel solution. Working as a grocery checkout clerk is mostly algorithmic. You do pretty much the same thing over and over in a certain way. Creating an ad campaign is mostly heuristic. You have to come up with something new.

During the twentieth century, most work was algorithmic—and not just jobs where you turned the same screw the same way all day long. Even when we traded blue collars for white, the tasks we carried out were often routine. That is, we could reduce much of what we did—in accounting, law, computer programming, and other fields—to a script, a spec sheet, a formula, or a series of steps that produced a right answer. But today, in much of North America, Western Europe, Japan, South Korea, and Australia, routine white-collar work is disappearing. It's racing offshore to wherever it can be done the cheapest. In India, Bulgaria, the Philippines, and other countries, lower-paid workers essentially run the algorithm, figure out the correct answer, and deliver it instantaneously from their computer to someone six thousand miles away.

But offshoring is just one pressure on rule-based, left-brain work. Just as oxen and then forklifts replaced simple physical labor, computers are replacing simple intellectual labor. So while outsourcing is just beginning to pick up speed, software can already perform many rule-based, professional functions better, more quickly, and more cheaply than we can. That means that your cousin the CPA, if he's doing mostly routine work, faces competition not just from five-hundred-dollar-a-month accountants in Manila, but from tax preparation programs anyone can download for thirty dollars. The consulting firm McKinsey & Co. estimates that in the United States, only 30 percent of job growth now comes from algorithmic work, while 70 percent comes from heuristic work.[9] A key reason: Routine work can be outsourced or automated; artistic, empathic, nonroutine work generally cannot.[10]

The implications for motivation are vast. Researchers such as Harvard Business School's Teresa Amabile have found that external rewards and punishments—both carrots and sticks—can work nicely for algorithmic tasks. But they can be devastating for heuristic ones. Those sorts of challenges—solving novel problems or creating something the world didn't know it was missing—depend heavily on Harlow's third drive. Amabile calls it the intrinsic motivation principle of creativity, which holds, in part: "Intrinsic motivation is conducive to creativity; controlling extrinsic motivation is detrimental to creativity."[11] In other words, the central tenets of Motivation 2.0 may actually *impair* performance of the heuristic, right-brain work on which modern economies depend.

Partly because work has become more creative and less routine, it has also become more enjoyable. That, too, scrambles Motivation 2.0's assumptions. This operating system rests on the belief that work is *not* inherently enjoyable—which is precisely why we must coax people with external rewards and threaten them with outside punishment. One unexpected finding of the psychologist Mihaly Csikszentmihalyi, whom we'll encounter in Chapter 5, is that people are much more likely to report having "optimal experiences" on the job than during leisure. But if work is inherently enjoyable for more and more people, then the external inducements at the heart of Motivation 2.0 become less necessary. Worse, as Deci began discovering forty years ago, adding certain kinds of extrinsic rewards on top of inherently interesting tasks can often dampen motivation and diminish performance.

Once again, certain bedrock notions suddenly seem less sturdy. Take the curious example of Vocation Vacations. This is a business in which people pay their hard-earned money . . . to work at another job. They use their vacation time to test-drive being a chef, running a bike shop, or operating an animal shelter. The emergence of this and similar ventures suggests that work, which economists have always considered a "disutility" (something we'd avoid unless we received a payment in return), is becoming a "utility" (something we'd pursue even in the absence of a tangible return).

Finally, because work is supposed to be dreary, Motivation 2.0 holds that people need to be carefully monitored so they don't shirk. This idea, too, is becoming less relevant and, in many ways, less possible. Consider, for instance, that America alone now has more than 18 million of what the U.S. Census Bureau calls "non-employer businesses"—businesses without any paid employees. Since people in these businesses don't have any underlings, they don't have anybody to manage or motivate. But since they don't have bosses themselves, there's nobody to manage or motivate them. They have to be self-directed.

So do people who aren't technically working for themselves. In the United States, 33.7 million people telecommute at least one day a month, and 14.7 million do so every day—placing a substantial portion of the workforce beyond the gaze of a manager, forcing them to direct their own work.[12] And even if many organizations haven't opted for measures like these, they're generally becoming leaner and less hierarchical. In an effort to reduce costs, they trim the fatty middle. That means managers oversee larger numbers of people and therefore scrutinize each one less closely.

As organizations flatten, companies need people who are self-motivated. That forces many organizations to become more like, er, Wikipedia. Nobody "manages" the Wikipedians. Nobody sits around trying to figure out how to "motivate" them. That's why Wikipedia works. Routine, not-so-interesting jobs require direction; non-routine, more interesting work depends on self-direction. One business leader, who didn't want to be identified, said it plainly. When he conducts job interviews, he tells prospective employees: "If you need me to motivate you, I probably don't want to hire you."

To RECAP, Motivation 2.0 suffers from three compatibility problems. It doesn't mesh with the way many new business models are organizing what we do—because we're intrinsically motivated purpose maximizers, not only extrinsically motivated profit maximizers. It doesn't comport with the way that twenty-first-century economics thinks about what we do—because economists are finally realizing that we're full-fledged human beings, not single-minded economic robots. And perhaps most important, it's hard to reconcile with much of what we actually do at work—because for growing numbers of people, work is often creative, interesting, and self-directed rather than unrelentingly routine, boring, and other-directed. Taken together, these compatibility problems warn us that something's gone awry in our motivational operating system.

But in order to figure out exactly what, and as an essential step in fashioning a new one, we need to take a look at the bugs themselves.

CHAPTER 2

Seven Reasons Carrots and Sticks (Often) Don't Work . . .

*A*n object in motion will stay in motion, and an object at rest will stay at rest, unless acted on by an outside force.

That's Newton's first law of motion. Like Newton's other laws, this one is elegant and simple—which is part of its power. Even people like me, who bumbled through high school physics, can understand it and can use it to interpret the world.

Motivation 2.0 is similar. At its heart are two elegant and simple ideas:

Rewarding an activity will get you more of it. Punishing an activity will get you less of it.

And just as Newton's principles can help us explain our physical environment or chart the path of a thrown ball, Motivation 2.0's principles can help us comprehend our social surroundings and predict the trajectory of human behavior.

But Newtonian physics runs into problems at the subatomic level. Down there—in the land of hadrons, quarks, and Schrödinger's cat—things get freaky. The cool rationality of Isaac Newton gives way to the bizarre unpredictability of Lewis Carroll. Motivation 2.0 is similar in this regard, too. When rewards and punishments encounter our third drive, something akin to behavioral quantum mechanics seems to take over and strange things begin to happen.

Of course, the starting point for any discussion of motivation in the workplace is a simple fact of life: People have to earn a living. Salary, contract payments, some benefits, a few perks are what I call "baseline rewards." If someone's baseline rewards aren't adequate or equitable, her focus will be on the unfairness of her situation and the anxiety of her circumstance. You'll get neither the predictability of extrinsic motivation nor the weirdness of intrinsic motivation. You'll get very little motivation at all.

But once we're past that threshold, carrots and sticks can achieve precisely the *opposite* of their intended aims. Mechanisms designed to increase motivation can dampen it. Tactics aimed at boosting creativity can reduce it. Programs to promote good deeds can make them disappear. Meanwhile, instead of restraining negative behavior, rewards and punishments can often set it loose—and give rise to cheating, addiction, and dangerously myopic thinking.

This is weird. And it doesn't hold in all circumstances (about which more after this chapter). But as Edward Deci's Soma puzzle experiment demonstrates, many practices whose effectiveness we take for granted produce counterintuitive results: They can give us less of what we want—and more of what we don't want. These are the bugs in Motivation 2.0. And they rise to the surface whether we're promising rupees in India, charging shekels in Israel, drawing blood in Sweden, or painting portraits in Chicago.

LESS OF WHAT WE WANT

One of the most enduring scenes in American literature offers an important lesson in human motivation. In Chapter 2 of Mark Twain's *The Adventures of Tom Sawyer*, Tom faces the dreary task of whitewashing Aunt Polly's 810-square-foot fence. He's not exactly thrilled with the assignment. "Life to him seemed hollow, and existence but a burden," Twain writes.

But just when Tom has nearly lost hope, "nothing less than a great, magnificent inspiration" bursts upon him. When his friend Ben ambles by and mocks Tom for his sorry lot, Tom acts confused. Slapping paint on a fence isn't a grim chore, he says. It's a fantastic privilege—a source of, ahem, intrinsic motivation. The job is so captivating that when Ben asks to try a few brushstrokes himself, Tom refuses. He doesn't relent until Ben gives up his apple in exchange for the opportunity.

Soon more boys arrive, all of whom tumble into Tom's trap and end up whitewashing the fence—several times over—on his behalf. From this episode, Twain extracts a key motivational principle, namely "that Work consists of whatever a body is OBLIGED to do, and that Play consists of whatever a body is not obliged to do." He goes on to write:

> There are wealthy gentlemen in England who drive four-horse passenger-coaches twenty or thirty miles on a daily line, in the summer, because the privilege costs them considerable money;

but if they were offered wages for the service, that would turn it into work and then they would resign.[1]

In other words, rewards can perform a weird sort of behavioral alchemy: They can transform an interesting task into a drudge. They can turn play into work. And by diminishing intrinsic motivation, they can send performance, creativity, and even upstanding behavior toppling like dominoes. Let's call this the Sawyer Effect.* A sampling of intriguing experiments around the world reveals the four realms where this effect kicks in—and shows yet again the mismatch between what science knows and what business does.

Intrinsic Motivation

Behavioral scientists like Deci began discovering the Sawyer Effect nearly forty years ago, although they didn't use that term. Instead, they referred to the counterintuitive consequences of extrinsic incentives as "the hidden costs of rewards." That, in fact, was the title of the first book on the subject—a 1978 research volume that was edited by psychologists Mark Lepper and David Greene.

One of Lepper and Greene's early studies (which they carried out with a third colleague, Robert Nisbett) has become a classic in the field and among the most cited articles in the motivation literature. The three researchers watched a classroom of preschoolers for several days and identified the children who chose to spend their "free play" time drawing. Then they fashioned an experiment to test the effect of rewarding an activity these children clearly enjoyed.

---

*Here's the two-sided definition of the Sawyer Effect: practices that can either turn play into work or turn work into play.

The researchers divided the children into three groups. The first was the "expected-award" group. They showed each of these children a "Good Player" certificate—adorned with a blue ribbon and featuring the child's name—and asked if the child wanted to draw in order to receive the award. The second group was the "unexpected-award" group. Researchers asked these children simply if they wanted to draw. If they decided to, when the session ended, the researchers handed each child one of the "Good Player" certificates. The third group was the "no-award" group. Researchers asked these children if they wanted to draw, but neither promised them a certificate at the beginning nor gave them one at the end.

Two weeks later, back in the classroom, teachers set out paper and markers during the preschool's free play period while the researchers secretly observed the students. Children previously in the "unexpected-award" and "no-award" groups drew just as much, and with the same relish, as they had before the experiment. But children in the first group—the ones who'd expected and then received an award—showed much less interest and spent much less time drawing.[2] The Sawyer Effect had taken hold. Even two weeks later, those alluring prizes—so common in classrooms and cubicles—had turned play into work.

To be clear, it wasn't necessarily the rewards themselves that dampened the children's interest. Remember: When children didn't expect a reward, receiving one had little impact on their intrinsic motivation. Only *contingent* rewards—if you do this, then you'll get that—had the negative effect. Why? "If-then" rewards require people to forfeit some of their autonomy. Like the gentlemen driving carriages for money instead of fun, they're no longer fully controlling their lives. And that can spring a hole in the bottom of their motivational bucket, draining an activity of its enjoyment.

Lepper and Greene replicated these results in several subsequent experiments with children. As time went on, other researchers found similar results with adults. Over and over again, they discovered that extrinsic rewards—in particular, contingent, expected, "if-then" rewards—snuffed out the third drive.

These insights proved so controversial—after all, they called into question a standard practice of most companies and schools—that in 1999 Deci and two colleagues reanalyzed nearly three decades of studies on the subject to confirm the findings. "Careful consideration of reward effects reported in 128 experiments lead to the conclusion that tangible rewards tend to have a substantially negative effect on intrinsic motivation," they determined. "When institutions— families, schools, businesses, and athletic teams, for example—focus on the short-term and opt for controlling people's behavior," they do considerable long-term damage.[3]

Try to encourage a kid to learn math by paying her for each workbook page she completes—and she'll almost certainly become more diligent in the short term and lose interest in math in the long term. Take an industrial designer who loves his work and try to get him to do better by making his pay contingent on a hit product—and he'll almost certainly work like a maniac in the short term, but become less interested in his job in the long term. As one leading behavioral science textbook puts it, "People use rewards expecting to gain the benefit of increasing another person's motivation and behavior, but in so doing, they often incur the unintentional and hidden cost of undermining that person's intrinsic motivation toward the activity."[4]

This is one of the most robust findings in social science—and also one of the most ignored. Despite the work of a few skilled and passionate popularizers—in particular, Alfie Kohn, whose prescient 1993 book, *Punished by Rewards*, lays out a devastating indictment of extrinsic incentives—we persist in trying to motivate people this way. Perhaps we're scared to let go of Motivation 2.0, despite its obvious downsides. Perhaps we can't get our minds around the peculiar quantum mechanics of intrinsic motivation.

Or perhaps there's a better reason. Even if those controlling "if-then" rewards activate the Sawyer Effect and suffocate the third drive, maybe they actually get people to perform better. If that's the case, perhaps they're not so bad. So let's ask: Do extrinsic rewards boost performance? Four economists went to India to find out.

High Performance

One of the difficulties of laboratory experiments that test the impact of extrinsic motivators like cash is the cost. If you're going to pay people to perform, you have to pay them a meaningful amount. And in the United States or Europe, where standards of living are high, an individually meaningful amount multiplied by dozens of participants can rack up unsustainably large bills for behavioral scientists.

In part to circumvent this problem, a quartet of economists—including Dan Ariely, whom I mentioned in the last chapter—set up shop in Madurai, India, to gauge the effects of extrinsic incentives on performance. Because the cost of living in rural India is much lower than in North America, the researchers could offer large rewards without breaking their own banks.

They recruited eighty-seven participants and asked them to play several games—for example, tossing tennis balls at a target, unscrambling anagrams, recalling a string of digits—that required motor skills, creativity, or concentration. To test the power of incentives, the experimenters offered three types of rewards for reaching certain performance levels.

One-third of the participants could earn a small reward—4 rupees (at the time worth around 50 U.S. cents and equal to about a day's pay in Madurai) for reaching their performance targets. One-third could earn a medium reward—40 rupees (about $5, or two weeks' pay). And one-third could earn a very large reward—400 rupees (about $50, or nearly five months' pay).

What happened? Did the size of the reward predict the quality of the performance?

Yes. But not in the way you might expect. As it turned out, the people offered the medium-sized bonus didn't perform any better than those offered the small one. And those in the 400-rupee super-incentivized group? They fared worst of all. By nearly every measure, they lagged behind both the low-reward and medium-reward participants. Reporting the results for the Federal Reserve Bank of Boston, the researchers wrote, "In eight of the nine tasks we examined across the three experiments, higher incentives led to *worse* performance."[5]

Let's circle back to this conclusion for a moment. Four economists—two from MIT, one from Carnegie Mellon, and one from the University of Chicago—undertake research for the Federal Reserve System, one of the most powerful economic actors in the world. But instead of affirming a simple business principle—higher rewards lead to higher performance—they seem to refute it. And it's not just American researchers reaching these counterintuitive conclusions. In 2009, scholars at the London School of Economics—alma mater of eleven Nobel laureates in economics—analyzed fifty-one studies of corporate pay-for-performance plans. These economists' conclusion: "We find that financial incentives . . . can result in a negative impact on overall performance."[6] On both sides of the Atlantic, the gap between what science is learning and what business is doing is wide.

"Many existing institutions provide very large incentives for exactly the type of tasks we used here," Ariely and his colleagues wrote. "Our results challenge [that] assumption. Our experiment suggests . . . that one cannot assume that introducing or raising incentives always improves performance." Indeed, in many instances, contingent incentives—that cornerstone of how businesses attempt to motivate employees—may be "a losing proposition."

Of course, procrastinating writers notwithstanding, few of us spend our working hours flinging tennis balls or doing anagrams. How about the more creative tasks that are more akin to what we actually do on the job?

Creativity

For a quick test of problem-solving prowess, few exercises are more useful than the "candle problem." Devised by psychologist Karl Duncker in the 1930s, the candle problem is used in a wide variety of experiments in behavioral science. Follow along and see how you do.

You sit at a table next to a wooden wall and the experimenter gives you the materials shown below: a candle, some tacks, and a book of matches.

The candle problem presented.

Your job is to attach the candle to the wall so that the wax doesn't drip on the table. Think for a moment about how you'd solve the problem. Many people begin by trying to tack the candle to the wall. But that doesn't work. Some light a match, melt the side of the candle, and try to adhere it to the wall. That doesn't work either. But after five or ten minutes, most people stumble onto the solution, which you can see below.

The candle problem solved.

The key is to overcome what's called "functional fixedness." You look at the box and see only one function—as a container for the tacks. But by thinking afresh, you eventually see that the box can have another function—as a platform for the candle. To reprise language from the previous chapter, the solution isn't algorithmic (following a set path) but heuristic (breaking from the path to discover a novel strategy).

What happens when you give people a conceptual challenge like this and offer them rewards for speedy solutions? Sam Glucksberg, a psychologist now at Princeton University, tested this a few decades ago by timing how quickly two groups of participants solved the candle problem. He told the first group that he was timing their work merely to establish norms for how long it typically took someone to complete this sort of puzzle. To the second group he offered incentives. If a participant's time was among the fastest 25 percent of all the people being tested, that participant would receive $5. If the participant's time was the fastest of all, the reward would be $20. Adjusted for inflation, those are decent sums of money for a few minutes of effort—a nice motivator.

How much faster did the incentivized group come up with a solution? On average, it took them nearly three and a half minutes *longer*.[7] Yes, three and a half minutes longer. (Whenever I've relayed these results to a group of businesspeople, the reaction is almost always a loud, pained, involuntary gasp.) In direct contravention to the core tenets of Motivation 2.0, an incentive designed to clarify thinking and sharpen creativity ended up clouding thinking and dulling creativity. Why? Rewards, by their very nature, narrow our focus. That's helpful when there's a clear path to a solution. They help us stare ahead and race faster. But "if-then" motivators are terrible for challenges like the candle problem. As this experiment shows, the rewards narrowed people's focus and blinkered the wide view that might have allowed them to see new uses for old objects.

Something similar seems to occur for challenges that aren't so much about cracking an existing problem but about iterating something new. Teresa Amabile, the Harvard Business School professor and one of the world's leading researchers on creativity, has frequently tested the effects of contingent rewards on the creative process. In one study, she and two colleagues recruited twenty-three professional artists from the United States who had produced both commissioned and noncommissioned artwork. They asked the artists to randomly select ten commissioned works and ten noncommissioned works. Then Amabile and her team gave the works to a panel of accomplished artists and curators, who knew nothing about the study, and asked the experts to rate the pieces on creativity and technical skill.

"Our results were quite startling," the researchers wrote. "The commissioned works were rated as significantly less creative than the non-commissioned works, yet they were not rated as different in technical quality. Moreover, the artists reported feeling significantly more constrained when doing commissioned works than when doing non-commissioned works." One artist whom they interviewed describes the Sawyer Effect in action:

> Not always, but a lot of the time, when you are doing a piece for someone else it becomes more "work" than joy. When I work for myself there is the pure joy of creating and I can work through the night and not even know it. On a commissioned piece you have to check yourself—be careful to do what the client wants.[8]

Another study of artists over a longer period shows that a concern for outside rewards might actually hinder eventual success. In the early 1960s, researchers surveyed sophomores and juniors at the School of the Art Institute of Chicago about their attitudes toward work and whether they were more intrinsically or extrinsically motivated. Using these data as a benchmark, another researcher followed up with these students in the early 1980s to see how their careers were progressing. Among the starkest findings, especially for men: "The less evidence of extrinsic motivation during art school, the more success in professional art both several years after graduation and nearly twenty years later." Painters and sculptors who were intrinsically motivated, those for whom the joy of discovery and the challenge of creation were their own rewards, were able to weather the tough times—and the lack of remuneration and recognition—that inevitably accompany artistic careers. And that led to yet another paradox in the Alice in Wonderland world of the third drive. "Those artists who pursued their painting and sculpture more for the pleasure of the activity itself than for extrinsic rewards have produced art that has been socially recognized as superior," the study said. "It is those who are least motivated to pursue extrinsic rewards who eventually receive them." [9]

This result is not true across all tasks, of course. Amabile and others have found that extrinsic rewards can be effective for algorithmic tasks—those that depend on following an existing formula to its logical conclusion. But for more right-brain undertakings—those that demand flexible problem-solving, inventiveness, or conceptual understanding—contingent rewards can be dangerous. Rewarded subjects often have a harder time seeing the periphery and crafting original solutions. This, too, is one of the sturdiest findings in social science—especially as Amabile and others have refined it over the years.[10] For artists, scientists, inventors, schoolchildren, and the rest of us, intrinsic motivation—the drive do something because it is interesting, challenging, and absorbing—is essential for high levels of creativity. But the "if-then" motivators that are the staple of most businesses often stifle, rather than stir, creative thinking. As the economy moves toward more right-brain, conceptual work—as more of us deal with our own versions of the candle problem—this might be the most alarming gap between what science knows and what business does.

Good Behavior

Philosophers and medical professionals have long debated whether blood donors should be paid. Some claim that blood, like human tissue or organs, is special—that we shouldn't be able to buy and sell it like a barrel of crude oil or a crate of ball bearings. Others argue that we should shelve our squeamishness, because paying for this substance will ensure an ample supply.

But in 1970, British sociologist Richard Titmuss, who had studied blood donation in the United Kingdom, offered a bolder speculation. Paying for blood wasn't just immoral, he said. It was also inefficient. If Britain decided to pay citizens to donate, that would actually *reduce* the country's blood supply. It was an oddball notion, to be sure. Economists snickered. And Titmuss never tested the idea; it was merely a philosophical hunch.[11]

But a quarter-century later, two Swedish economists decided to see if Titmuss was right. In an intriguing field experiment, they visited a regional blood center in Gothenburg and found 153 women who were interested in giving blood. Then—as seems to be the custom among motivation researchers—they divided the women into three groups.[12] Experimenters told those in the first group that blood donation was voluntary. These participants could give blood, but they wouldn't receive a payment. The experimenters offered the second group a different arrangement. If these participants gave blood, they'd each receive 50 Swedish kronor (about $7). The third group received a variation on that second offer: a 50-kronor payment with an immediate option to donate the amount to a children's cancer charity.

Of the first group, 52 percent of the women decided to go ahead and donate blood. They were altruistic citizens apparently, willing to do a good deed for their fellow Swedes even in the absence of compensation.

And the second group? Motivation 2.0 would suggest that this group might be a bit more motivated to donate. They'd shown up, which indicated intrinsic motivation. Getting a few kronor on top might give that impulse a boost. But—as you might have guessed by now—that's not what happened. In this group, only 30 percent of the women decided to give blood. Instead of increasing the number of blood donors, offering to pay people *decreased* the number by nearly half.

Meanwhile, the third group—which had the option of donating the fee directly to charity—responded much the same as the first group. Fifty-three percent became blood donors.*

Titmuss's hunch might have been right, after all. Adding a monetary incentive didn't lead to more of the desired behavior. It led to less. The reason: It tainted an altruistic act and "crowded out" the intrinsic desire to do something good.[13] Doing good is what blood donation is all about. It provides what the American Red Cross brochures say is "a feeling that money can't buy." That's why voluntary blood donations invariably increase during natural disasters and other calamities.[14] But if governments were to pay people to help their neighbors during these crises, donations might decline.

That said, in the Swedish example, the reward itself wasn't inherently destructive. The immediate option to donate the 50-kronor payment rather than pocket it seemed to negate the effect. This, too, is extremely important. It's not that all rewards at all times are bad. For instance, when the Italian government gave blood donors paid

---

*The results for the 119 men in the experiment were somewhat different. The payment had no statistically significant effect, positive or negative, on the decision to give blood.

time off work, donations increased.[15] The law removed an obstacle to altruism. So while a few advocates would have you believe in the basic evil of extrinsic incentives, that's just not empirically true. What is true is that mixing rewards with inherently interesting, creative, or noble tasks—deploying them without understanding the peculiar science of motivation—is a very dangerous game. When used in these situations, "if-then" rewards usually do more harm than good. By neglecting the ingredients of genuine motivation—autonomy, mastery, and purpose—they limit what each of us can achieve.

MORE OF WHAT WE DON'T WANT

In the upside-down universe of the third drive, rewards can often produce less of the very things they're trying to encourage. But that's not the end of the story. When used improperly, extrinsic motivators can have another unintended collateral consequence: They can give us more of what we don't want. Here, again, what business does hasn't caught up with what science knows. And what science is revealing is that carrots and sticks can promote bad behavior, create addiction, and encourage short-term thinking at the expense of the long view.

Unethical Behavior

What could be more valuable than having a goal? From our earliest days, teachers, coaches, and parents advise us to set goals and to work mightily to achieve them—and with good reason. Goals work. The academic literature shows that by helping us tune out distractions, goals can get us to try harder, work longer, and achieve more.

But recently a group of scholars from the Harvard Business School, Northwestern University's Kellogg School of Management, the University of Arizona's Eller College of Management, and the University of Pennsylvania's Wharton School questioned the efficacy of this broad prescription. "Rather than being offered as an 'over-the-counter' salve for boosting performance, goal setting should be prescribed selectively, presented with a warning label, and closely monitored," they wrote.[16] Goals that people set for themselves and that are devoted to attaining mastery are usually healthy. But goals imposed by others—sales targets, quarterly returns, standardized test scores, and so on—can sometimes have dangerous side effects.

Like all extrinsic motivators, goals narrow our focus. That's one reason they can be effective; they concentrate the mind. But as we've seen, a narrowed focus exacts a cost. For complex or conceptual tasks, offering a reward can blinker the wide-ranging thinking necessary to come up with an innovative solution. Likewise, when an extrinsic goal is paramount—particularly a short-term, measurable one whose achievement delivers a big payoff—its presence can restrict our view of the broader dimensions of our behavior. As the cadre of business school professors write, "Substantial evidence demonstrates that in addition to motivating constructive effort, goal setting can induce unethical behavior."

The examples are legion, the researchers note. Sears imposes a sales quota on its auto repair staff—and workers respond by over-charging customers and completing unnecessary repairs. Enron sets lofty revenue goals—and the race to meet them by any means possible catalyzes the company's collapse. Ford is so intent on producing a certain car at a certain weight at a certain price by a certain date that it omits safety checks and unleashes the dangerous Ford Pinto.

The problem with making an extrinsic reward the only destination that matters is that some people will choose the quickest route there, even if it means taking the low road.

Indeed, most of the scandals and misbehavior that have seemed endemic to modern life involve shortcuts. Executives game their quarterly earnings so they can snag a performance bonus. Secondary school counselors doctor student transcripts so their seniors can get into college.[17] Athletes inject themselves with steroids to post better numbers and trigger lucrative performance bonuses.

Contrast that approach with behavior sparked by intrinsic motivation. When the reward is the activity itself—deepening learning, delighting customers, doing one's best—there are no shortcuts. The only route to the destination is the high road. In some sense, it's impossible to act unethically because the person who's disadvantaged isn't a competitor but yourself.

Of course, all goals are not created equal. And—let me emphasize this point—goals and extrinsic rewards aren't inherently corrupting. But goals are more toxic than Motivation 2.0 recognizes. In fact, the business school professors suggest they should come with their own warning label: *Goals may cause systematic problems for organizations due to narrowed focus, unethical behavior, increased risk taking, decreased cooperation, and decreased intrinsic motivation. Use care when applying goals in your organization.*

If carrots-as-goals sometimes encourage unworthy behavior, then sticks-as-punishment should be able to halt it, right? Not so fast. The third drive is less mechanistic and more surprising than that, as two Israeli economists discovered at some day care centers.

In 2000, economists Uri Gneezy and Aldo Rustichini studied a group of child care facilities in Haifa, Israel, for twenty weeks.[18] The centers opened at 7:30 A.M. and closed at 4:00 P.M. Parents had to retrieve their children by the closing time or a teacher would have to stay late.

During the first four weeks of the experiment, the economists recorded how many parents arrived late each week. Then, before the fifth week, with the permission of the day care centers, they posted the following sign:

ANNOUNCEMENT:
FINE FOR COMING LATE

As you all know, the official closing time of the day care center is 1600 every day. Since some parents have been coming late, we (with the approval of the Authority for Private Day-Care Centers in Israel) have decided to impose a fine on parents who come late to pick up their children.

As of next Sunday a fine of NS 10* will be charged every time a child is collected after 1610. This fine will be calculated monthly, it is to be paid together with the regular monthly payment.

Sincerely,

The manager of the day-care center

The theory underlying the fine, said Gneezy and Rustichini, was straightforward: "When negative consequences are imposed on a behavior, they will produce a reduction of that particular response." In other words, thwack the parents with a fine, and they'll stop showing up late.

---

*The fine was per child, so a parent with two children would have to pay twenty Israeli shekels (NS 20) for each instance of tardiness. When the experiment was conducted, ten Israeli shekels was equivalent to about three U.S. dollars.

But that's not what happened. "After the introduction of the fine we observed a steady *increase* in the number of parents coming late," the economists wrote. "The rate finally settled, at a level that was higher, and *almost twice as large* as the initial one."[19] And in language reminiscent of Harry Harlow's head scratching, they write that the existing literature didn't account for such a result. Indeed, the "possibility of an increase in the behavior being punished was not even considered."

Up pops another bug in Motivation 2.0. One reason most parents showed up on time is that they had a relationship with the teachers—who, after all, were caring for their precious sons and daughters—and wanted to treat them fairly. Parents had an intrinsic desire to be scrupulous about punctuality. But the threat of a fine—like the promise of the kronor in the blood experiment—edged aside that third drive. The fine shifted the parents' decision from a partly moral obligation (be fair to my kids' teachers) to a pure transaction (I can buy extra time). There wasn't room for both. The punishment didn't promote good behavior; it crowded it out.

Addiction

If some scientists believe that "if-then" motivators and other extrinsic rewards resemble prescription drugs that carry potentially dangerous side effects, others believe they're more like illegal drugs that foster a deeper and more pernicious dependency. According to these scholars, cash rewards and shiny trophies can provide a delicious jolt of pleasure at first, but the feeling soon dissipates—and to keep it alive, the recipient requires ever larger and more frequent doses.

The Russian economist Anton Suvorov has constructed an

elaborate econometric model to demonstrate this effect, configured around what's called "principal-agent theory." Think of the principal as the motivator—the employer, the teacher, the parent. Think of the agent as the motivatee—the employee, the student, the child. A principal essentially tries to get the agent to do what the principal wants, while the agent balances his own interests with whatever the principal is offering. Using a blizzard of complicated equations that test a variety of scenarios between principal and agent, Suvorov has reached conclusions that make intuitive sense to any parent who's tried to get her kids to empty the garbage.

By offering a reward, a principal signals to the agent that the task is undesirable. (If the task were desirable, the agent wouldn't need a prod.) But that initial signal, and the reward that goes with it, forces the principal onto a path that's difficult to leave. Offer too small a reward and the agent won't comply. But offer a reward that's enticing enough to get the agent to act the first time, and the principal "is doomed to give it again in the second." There's no going back. Pay your son to take out the trash—and you've pretty much guaranteed the kid will never do it again for free. What's more, once the initial money buzz tapers off, you'll likely have to increase the payment to continue compliance.

As Suvorov explains, "Rewards are addictive in that once offered, a contingent reward makes an agent expect it whenever a similar task is faced, which in turn compels the principal to use rewards over and over again." And before long, the existing reward may no longer suffice. It will quickly feel less like a bonus and more like the status quo—which then forces the principal to offer larger rewards to achieve the same effect.[20]

This addictive pattern is not merely blackboard theory. Brian Knutson, then a neuroscientist at the National Institute on Alcohol

Abuse and Alcoholism, demonstrated as much in an experiment using the brain scanning technique known as functional magnetic resonance imaging (fMRI). He placed healthy volunteers into a giant scanner to watch how their brains responded during a game that involved the prospect of either winning or losing money. When participants knew they had a chance to win cash, activation occurred in the part of the brain called the nucleus accumbens. That is, when the participants anticipated getting a reward (but not when they anticipated losing one), a burst of the brain chemical dopamine surged to this part of the brain. Knutson, who is now at Stanford University, has found similar results in subsequent studies where people anticipated rewards. What makes this response interesting for our purposes is that the same basic physiological process—this particular brain chemical surging to this particular part of the brain—is what happens in addiction. The mechanism of most addictive drugs is to send a fusillade of dopamine to the nucleus accumbens. The feeling delights, then dissipates, then demands another dose. In other words, if we watch how people's brains respond, promising them monetary rewards and giving them cocaine, nicotine, or amphetamines look disturbingly similar.[21] This could be one reason that paying people to stop smoking often works in the short run. It replaces one (dangerous) addiction with another (more benign) one.

Rewards' addictive qualities can also distort decision-making. Knutson has found that activation in the nucleus accumbens seems to predict "both risky choices and risk-seeking mistakes." Get people fired up with the prospect of rewards, and instead of making better decisions, as Motivation 2.0 hopes, they can actually make worse ones. As Knutson writes, "This may explain why casinos surround their guests with reward cues (e.g., inexpensive food, free liquor, surprise gifts, potential jackpot prizes)—anticipation of rewards activates the [nucleus accumbens], which may lead to an increase in the likelihood of individuals switching from risk-averse to risk-seeking behavior."[22]

In short, while that dangled carrot isn't all bad in all circumstances, in some instances it operates similar to a rock of crack cocaine and can induce behavior similar to that found around the craps table or roulette wheel—not exactly what we hope to achieve when we "motivate" our teammates and coworkers.

Short-Term Thinking

Think back to the candle problem again. The incentivized participants performed worse than their counterparts because they were so focused on the prize that they failed to glimpse a novel solution on the periphery. Rewards, we've seen, can limit the *breadth* of our thinking. But extrinsic motivators—especially tangible, "if-then" ones—can also reduce the *depth* of our thinking. They can focus our sights on only what's immediately before us rather than what's off in the distance.

Many times a concentrated focus makes sense. If your office building is on fire, you want to find an exit immediately rather than ponder how to rewrite the zoning regulations. But in less dramatic circumstances, fixating on an immediate reward can damage performance over time. Indeed, what our earlier examples—unethical actions and addictive behavior—have in common, perhaps more than anything else, is that they're entirely short-term. Addicts want the quick fix regardless of the eventual harm. Cheaters want the quick win—regardless of the lasting consequences.

Yet even when the behavior doesn't devolve into shortcuts or addiction, the near-term allure of rewards can be harmful in the long run. Consider publicly held companies. Many such companies have existed for decades and hope to exist for decades more. But much of what their executives and middle managers do each day is aimed single-mindedly at the corporation's performance over the next three months. At these companies, quarterly earnings are an obsession. Executives devote substantial resources to making sure the earnings come out just right. And they spend considerable time and brain-power offering guidance to stock analysts so that the market knows what to expect and therefore responds favorably. This laser focus on a narrow, near-term slice of corporate performance is understand-able. It's a rational response to stock markets that reward or pun-ish tiny blips in those numbers, which, in turn, affect executives' compensation.

But companies pay a steep price for not extending their gaze beyond the next quarter. Several researchers have found that com-panies that spend the most time offering guidance on quarterly earnings deliver significantly *lower* long-term growth rates than companies that offer guidance less frequently. (One reason: The earnings-obsessed companies typically invest less in research and development.)[23] They successfully achieve their short-term goals, but threaten the health of the company two or three years hence. As the scholars who warned about goals gone wild put it, "The very pres-ence of goals may lead employees to focus myopically on short-term gains and to lose sight of the potential devastating long-term effects on the organization."[24]

Perhaps nowhere is this clearer than in the economic calamity that gripped the world economy in 2008 and 2009. Each player in the system focused only on the short-term reward—the buyer who wanted a house, the mortgage broker who wanted a commission, the Wall Street trader who wanted new securities to sell, the politician who wanted a buoyant economy during reelection—and ignored the long-term effects of their actions on themselves or others. When the music stopped, the entire system nearly collapsed. This is the nature of economic bubbles: What seems to be irrational exuberance is ultimately a bad case of extrinsically motivated myopia.

By contrast, the elements of genuine motivation that we'll explore later, by their very nature, defy a short-term view. Take mastery. The objective itself is inherently long-term because complete mastery, in a sense, is unattainable. Even Roger Federer, for instance, will never fully "master" the game of tennis. But introducing an "if-then" reward to help develop mastery usually backfires. That's why school-children who are paid to solve problems typically choose easier problems and therefore learn less.[25] The short-term prize crowds out the long-term learning.

In environments where extrinsic rewards are most salient, many people work only to the point that triggers the reward—and no further. So if students get a prize for reading three books, many won't pick up a fourth, let alone embark on a lifetime of reading—just as executives who hit their quarterly numbers often won't boost earnings a penny more, let alone contemplate the long-term health of their company. Likewise, several studies show that paying people to exercise, stop smoking, or take their medicines produces terrific results at first—but the healthy behavior disappears once the incentives are removed. However, when contingent rewards aren't involved, or when incentives are used with the proper deftness, performance improves and understanding deepens. Greatness and near-sightedness are incompatible. Meaningful achievement depends on lifting one's sights and pushing toward the horizon.

CARROTS AND STICKS: *The Seven Deadly Flaws*

1. They can extinguish intrinsic motivation.
2. They can diminish performance.
3. They can crush creativity.
4. They can crowd out good behavior.
5. They can encourage cheating, shortcuts, and unethical behavior.
6. They can become addictive.
7. They can foster short-term thinking.

...and the Special Circumstances
When They Do

Carrots and sticks aren't all bad. If they were, Motivation 2.0 would never have flourished so long or accomplished so much. While an operating system centered around rewards and punishments has outlived its usefulness and badly needs an upgrade, that doesn't mean we should scrap its every piece. Indeed, doing so would run counter to the science. The scholars exploring human motivation have revealed not only the many glitches in the traditional approach, but also the narrow band of circumstances in which carrots and sticks do their jobs reasonably well.

The starting point, of course, is to ensure that the baseline rewards—wages, salaries, benefits, and so on—are adequate and fair. Without a healthy baseline, motivation of any sort is difficult and often impossible.

But once that's established, there are circumstances where it's okay to fall back on extrinsic motivators. To understand what those circumstances are, let's return to the candle problem. In his study, Sam Glucksberg found that the participants who were offered a cash prize took longer to solve the problem than those working in a reward-free environment. The reason, you'll recall, is that the prospect of a prize narrowed participants' focus and limited their ability to see an inventive, nonobvious solution.

In the same experiment, Glucksberg presented a separate set of participants with a slightly different version of the problem. Once again, he told half of them he was timing their performance to collect data—and the other half that those who posted the fastest times could win cash. But he altered things just a bit. Instead of giving participants a box full of tacks, he emptied the tacks onto the desk as shown below.

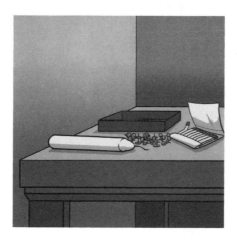

The candle problem presented differently.

Can you guess what happened?

This time, the participants vying for the reward solved the problem *faster* than their counterparts. Why? By removing the tacks and displaying the empty box, Glucksberg essentially revealed the solution. He transformed a challenging right-brain task into a routine left-brain one. Since participants simply had to race down an obvious path, the carrot waiting for them at the finish line encouraged them to gallop faster.

Glucksberg's experiment provides the first question you should ask when contemplating external motivators: *Is the task at hand routine?* That is, does accomplishing it require following a prescribed set of rules to a specified end?

For routine tasks, which aren't very interesting and don't demand much creative thinking, rewards can provide a small motivational booster shot without the harmful side effects. In some ways, that's just common sense. As Edward Deci, Richard Ryan, and Richard Koestner explain, "Rewards do not undermine people's intrinsic motivation for dull tasks because there is little or no intrinsic motivation to be undermined."[1] Likewise, when Dan Ariely and his colleagues conducted their Madurai, India, performance study with a group of MIT students, they found that when the task called for "even rudimentary cognitive skill," a larger reward "led to poorer performance." But "as long as the task involved only mechanical skill, bonuses worked as they would be expected: the higher the pay, the better the performance."[2]

This is extremely important. Although advanced economies now revolve less around those algorithmic, rule-based functions, some of what we do each day—especially on the job—still isn't all that interesting. We have TPS reports to fill out and boring e-mail to answer and all manner of drudge work that doesn't necessarily fire our soul. What's more, for some people, much of what they do *all day* consists of these routine, not terribly captivating, tasks. In these situations, it's best to try to unleash the positive side of the Sawyer Effect by attempting to turn work into play—to increase the task's variety, to make it more like a game, or to use it to help master other skills.

Alas, that's not always possible. And this means that sometimes, even "if-then" rewards are an option.

Let's put this insight about rewards and routines into practice. Suppose you're a manager at a small nonprofit organization. Your design team created a terrific poster promoting your group's next big event. And now you need to send the poster to twenty thousand members of your organization. Since the costs of outsourcing the job to a professional mailing firm are too steep for your budget, you decide to do the work in-house. Trouble is, the posters came back from the printer much later than you expected and they need to get in the mail this weekend.

What's the best way to enlist your staff of ten, and maybe a few others, in a massive weekend poster mailing session? The task is the very definition of routine: The people participating must roll up the posters, slide them into the mailing tubes, cap those tubes, and apply a mailing label and the proper postage. Four steps—none of them notably interesting.

One managerial option is coercion. If you're the boss, you could force people to spend their Saturday and Sunday on this mind-numbing project. They might comply, but the damage to their morale and long-term commitment could be substantial. Another option is to ask for volunteers. But face it: Most people can think of far better ways to spend a weekend.

So in this case, an "if-then" reward might be effective. For instance, you could promise a big office-wide party if everybody pitches in on the project. You could offer a gift certificate to everyone who participates. Or you could go further and pay people a small sum for every poster they insert, enclose, and send—in the hope that the piecework fee will boost their productivity.

While such tangible, contingent rewards can often undermine intrinsic motivation and creativity, those drawbacks matter less here. The assignment neither inspires deep passion nor requires deep thinking. Carrots, in this case, won't hurt and might help. And you'll increase your chances of success by supplementing the poster-packing rewards with three important practices:

- **Offer a rationale for why the task is necessary.** A job that's not inherently interesting can become more meaningful, and therefore more engaging, if it's part of a larger purpose. Explain why this poster is so important and why sending it out now is critical to your organization's mission.
- **Acknowledge that the task is boring.** This is an act of empathy, of course. And the acknowledgment will help people understand why this is the rare instance when "if-then" rewards are part of how your organization operates.
- **Allow people to complete the task their own way.** Think autonomy, not control. State the outcome you need. But instead of specifying precisely the way to reach it—how each poster must be rolled and how each mailing label must be affixed—give them freedom over how they do the job.

That's the approach for routine tasks. What about for other sorts of undertakings?

For work that requires more than just climbing, rung by rung, up a ladder of instructions, rewards are more perilous. The best way to avoid the seven deadly flaws of extrinsic motivators is to avoid them altogether or to downplay them significantly and instead emphasize the elements of deeper motivation—autonomy, mastery, and purpose—that we'll explore later in the book. But in the workplace, a rigid adherence to this approach bumps up against a fact of life: Even people who do groovy, creative, right-brain work still want to be paid. And here Teresa Amabile has shed some light on how to use rewards in a way that reckons with life's realities but reduces extrinsic motivators' hidden costs.

Go back to the study in which Amabile and two colleagues compared the quality of commissioned and noncommissioned paintings from a group of artists. A panel of experts, blind to what the investigators were exploring, consistently rated the noncommissioned artwork as more creative. One reason is that several artists said their commissions were "constraining"—that they found themselves working toward a goal they didn't endorse in a manner they didn't control. However, in the same study, Amabile also discovered that when the artists considered their commissions "enabling"—that is, "the commission enabled the artist to do something interesting or exciting"[3]—the creativity ranking of what they produced shot back up. The same was true for commissions the artists felt provided them with useful information and feedback about their ability.

This is a crucial research insight. The science shows that it is possible—though tricky—to incorporate rewards into nonroutine, more creative settings without causing a cascade of damage.

So suppose we're back at your nonprofit nine months later. The mailing went out flawlessly. The poster was a hit. The event was a smash. You're planning another for later this year. You've settled on the date and found your venue. Now you need an inspiring poster to captivate imaginations and draw a crowd.

What should you do?

Here's what you *shouldn't* do: Offer an "if-then" reward to the design staff. Do not stride into their offices and announce: "If you come up with a poster that rocks my world or that boosts attendance over last year, then you'll get a ten-percent bonus." Although that motivational approach is common in organizations all over the world, it's a recipe for reduced performance. Creating a poster isn't routine. It requires conceptual, breakthrough, artistic thinking. And as we've learned, "if-then" rewards are an ideal way to squash this sort of thinking.

Your best approach is to have already established the conditions of a genuinely motivating environment. The baseline rewards must be sufficient. That is, the team's basic compensation must be adequate and fair—particularly compared with people doing similar work for similar organizations. Your nonprofit must be a congenial place to work. And the people on your team must have autonomy, they must have ample opportunity to pursue mastery, and their daily duties must relate to a larger purpose. If these elements are in place, the best strategy is to provide a sense of urgency and significance—and then get out of the talent's way.

But you may still be able to boost performance a bit—more for future tasks than for this one—through the delicate use of rewards. Just be careful. Your efforts will backfire unless the rewards you offer meet one essential requirement. And you'll be on firmer motivational footing if you follow two additional principles.

The essential requirement: *Any extrinsic reward should be unexpected and offered only after the task is complete.*

Holding out a prize at the beginning of a project—and offering it as a contingency—will inevitably focus people's attention on obtaining the reward rather than on attacking the problem. But introducing the subject of rewards after the job is done is less risky.

In other words, where "if-then" rewards are a mistake, shift to "now that" rewards—as in "Now that you've finished the poster and it turned out so well, I'd like to celebrate by taking you out to lunch."

As Deci and his colleagues explain, "If tangible rewards are given unexpectedly to people after they have finished a task, the rewards are less likely to be experienced as the reason for doing the task and are thus less likely to be detrimental to intrinsic motivation."[4]

Likewise, Amabile has found in some studies "that the highest levels of creativity were produced by subjects who received a reward as a kind of a bonus."[5] So when the poster turns out great, you could buy the design team a case of beer or even hand them a cash bonus without snuffing their creativity. The team didn't expect any extras and getting them didn't hinge on a particular outcome. You're simply offering your appreciation for their stellar work. But keep in mind one ginormous caveat: Repeated "now that" bonuses can quickly become expected "if-then" entitlements—which can ultimately crater effective performance.

At this point, by limiting rewards for nonroutine, creative work to the unexpected, "now that" variety, you're in less dangerous waters. But you'll do even better if you follow two more guidelines.

First, *consider nontangible rewards*. Praise and positive feedback are much less corrosive than cash and trophies. In fact, in Deci's original experiments, and in his subsequent analysis of other studies, he found that "positive feedback can have an enhancing effect on intrinsic motivation."[6] So if the folks on the design team turn out a show-stopping poster, maybe just walk into their offices and say, "Wow. You really did an amazing job on that poster. It's going to have a huge impact on getting people to come to this event. Thank you." It sounds small and simple, but it can have an enormous effect.

Second, *provide useful information*. Amabile has found that while controlling extrinsic motivators can clobber creativity, "informational or enabling motivators can be conducive" to it.[7] In the workplace, people are thirsting to learn about how they're doing, but only if the information isn't a tacit effort to manipulate their behavior. So don't tell the design team: "That poster was perfect. You did it exactly the way I asked." Instead, give people meaningful information about their work. The more feedback focuses on specifics ("great use of color")—and the more the praise is about effort and strategy rather than about achieving a particular outcome—the more effective it can be.

In brief, for creative, right-brain, heuristic tasks, you're on shaky ground offering "if-then" rewards. You're better off using "now that" rewards. And you're best off if your "now that" rewards provide praise, feedback, and useful information.

(For a visual depiction of this approach, see the flowchart on the next page.)

When to Use Rewards: A Simple Flowchart

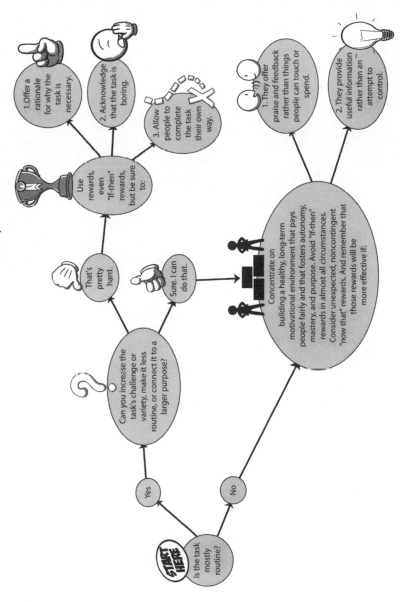

CHAPTER 3

Type I and Type X

Rochester, New York, is an unlikely epicenter for a social earth-quake. The companies that built this stolid city, just sixty-two miles from the Canadian border, were titans of the industrial economy. Eastman Kodak made film. Western Union delivered telegrams. Xerox produced photocopiers. And they piloted their enterprises by the precepts of Motivation 2.0: If you offer people steady employment and carefully calibrated rewards, they'll do what executives and shareholders want, and everyone will prosper.

But starting in the 1970s, on the campus of the University of Rochester, a motivational revolution was brewing. It began in 1971, when Edward Deci, fresh from his Soma puzzle experiments, arrived on campus for a joint appointment in the psychology department and the business school. It intensified in 1973, when the business school unceremoniously booted Deci because of his heretical findings about rewards, and the psychology department hired him full-time. It gathered more steam in 1975, when Deci published a book called *Intrinsic Motivation*. And it launched in earnest in 1977, when a student named Richard Ryan showed up for graduate school.

Ryan, a philosophy major in college, had just missed being drafted into the military. Nursing a bit of survivor's guilt, he'd been working with Vietnam War veterans suffering from post-traumatic stress disorder. And he'd come to the University of Rochester to learn how to become a better clinician. One day, in a seminar, a professor brought up the subject of intrinsic motivation—and then denounced it with table-pounding ferocity. "I figured that if there was that much resistance, this must be something interesting," Ryan told me. He picked up a copy of Deci's book, found it compelling, and asked its author to lunch. So commenced a remarkable research collaboration that continues to this day.

When I met them not long ago, in U of R's blocky Meliora Hall, the two were a study in both contrast and similarity. Deci is tall and reedy, with a pale complexion and thin, wispy hair. He speaks in a quiet, soothing voice that reminded me of the late American children's television host Mr. Rogers. Ryan, who has straight white hair parted down the middle, is ruddier and more intense. He presses his point like a skilled litigator. Deci, meanwhile, waits patiently for you to reach his point—then he agrees with you and praises your insight. Deci is the classical music station on your FM dial; Ryan is more cable TV. And yet they talk to each other in a cryptic academic shorthand, their ideas smoothly in sync. The combination has been powerful enough to make them among the most influential behavioral scientists of their generation.

Together Deci and Ryan have fashioned what they call "self-determination theory."

Many theories of behavior pivot around a particular human

tendency: We're keen responders to positive and negative reinforcements, or zippy calculators of our self-interest, or lumpy duffel bags of psychosexual conflicts. SDT, by contrast, begins with a notion of universal human *needs*. It argues that we have three innate psychological needs—competence, autonomy, and relatedness. When those needs are satisfied, we're motivated, productive, and happy. When they're thwarted, our motivation, productivity, and happiness plummet.[1] "If there's anything [fundamental] about our nature, it's the capacity for interest. Some things facilitate it. Some things undermine it," Ryan explained during one of our conversations. Put another way, we've all got that third drive. It's part of what it means to be human. But whether that aspect of our humanity emerges in our lives depends on whether the conditions around us support it.

And the main mechanisms of Motivation 2.0 are more stifling than supportive. "This is a really big thing in management," says Ryan. When people aren't producing, companies typically resort to rewards or punishment. "What you haven't done is the hard work of diagnosing what the problem is. You're trying to run over the problem with a carrot or a stick," Ryan explains. That doesn't mean that SDT unequivocally opposes rewards. "Of course, they're necessary in workplaces and other settings," says Deci. "But the less salient they are made, the better. When people use rewards to motivate, that's when they're most demotivating." Instead, Deci and Ryan say we should focus our efforts on creating environments for our innate psychological needs to flourish.

Over the last thirty years, through both their scholarship and mentorship, Deci and Ryan have established a network of several dozen SDT scholars conducting research in the United States, Canada, Israel, Singapore, and throughout Western Europe. These scientists have explored self-determination and intrinsic motivation in laboratory experiments and field studies that encompass just about every realm—business, education, medicine, sports, exercise, personal productivity, environmentalism, relationships, and physical and mental health. They have produced hundreds of research papers, most of which point to the same conclusion. Human beings have an innate inner drive to be autonomous, self-determined, and connected to one another. And when that drive is liberated, people achieve more and live richer lives.

SDT is an important part of a broad swirl of new thinking about the human condition. This constellation includes, perhaps most prominently, the positive psychology movement, which has reoriented the study of psychological science away from its previous focus on malady and dysfunction and toward well-being and effective functioning. Under the leadership of the University of Pennsylvania's Martin Seligman, positive psychology has been minting legions of new scholars and leaving a deep imprint on how scientists, economists, therapists, and everyday people think about human behavior. One of positive psychology's most influential figures is Mihaly Csikszentmihalyi, whom I mentioned earlier. Csikszentmihalyi's first book about "flow" and Seligman's first book on his theories (which argued that helplessness was learned, rather than innate, behavior) appeared in the same year as Deci's book on intrinsic motivation. Clearly, something big was in the air in 1975. It's just taken us a generation to reckon with it.

The broad assortment of new thinkers includes Carol Dweck of Stanford University and Harvard's Amabile. It includes a few economists—most prominently, Roland Bénabou of Princeton University and Bruno Frey of the University of Zurich—who are applying some of these concepts to the dismal science. And it includes some scholars who don't study motivation per se—in particular, Harvard University's Howard Gardner and Tufts University's Robert

Sternberg—who have changed our view of intelligence and creativity and offered a brighter view of human potential.

This collection of scholars—not in concert, not intentionally, and perhaps not even knowing they've been doing so—has been creating the foundation for a new, more effective, operating system. At long last, the times may be catching up to their work.

THE POWER OF THE ALPHABET

Words matter, of course, but so do letters. Case in point: Meyer Friedman. You've probably never heard of him, but you almost certainly know his legacy. Friedman, who died in 2001 at the ripe old age of ninety, was a cardiologist who for decades ran a bustling office in San Francisco. In the late 1950s, he and fellow physician Ray Rosenman began noticing similarities in their patients who were prone to heart disease. It wasn't only what these patients ate or what genes they inherited that affected their susceptibility to coronary trouble. It was also how they led their lives. These patients, Friedman noted, demonstrated:

> a particular complex of personality traits, including excessive competition drive, aggressiveness, impatience, and a harrying sense of time urgency. Individuals displaying this pattern seem to be engaged in a chronic, ceaseless, and often fruitless struggle—with themselves, with others, with circumstances, with time, sometimes with life itself.[2]

These people were significantly more likely to develop heart disease than other patients—even those who shared similar physical attributes, exercise regimens, diets, and family histories. Looking for a convenient and memorable way to explain this insight to their medical colleagues and the wider world, Friedman and Rosenman found inspiration in the alphabet. They dubbed this behavioral pattern "Type A."

Type A behavior stood in contrast to—natch—Type B behavior. Unlike their horn-honking, foot-tapping counterparts, who suffered from "hurry sickness," people displaying Type B behavior were rarely harried by life or made hostile by its demands. In their research, Friedman and Rosenman found that Type B people were just as intelligent, and frequently just as ambitious, as Type A's. But they wore their ambition differently. Writing about the Type B person (and using the male-centered language common in the day), the cardiologists explained, "He may also have a considerable amount of 'drive,' but its character is such that it seems to steady him, give confidence and security to him, rather than to goad, irritate, and infuriate, as with the Type A man."[3] One key to reducing deaths from heart disease and improving public health, therefore, was to help Type A's learn to become a little more like Type B's.

Nearly fifty years later, this nomenclature remains. The two letters help us understand a complex web of behaviors—and guide us toward a better and more effective way to live.

Around the same time that Friedman and Rosenman were making their discovery, another American was pushing frontiers of his own. Douglas McGregor was a management professor at MIT who brought to the job an interesting combination of experiences. He'd earned a Ph.D. from Harvard in psychology (rather than in economics or engineering). And in contrast to most of his colleagues, he'd actually run an institution. From 1948 to 1954, he was president of Antioch College.

Drawing on his understanding of the human psyche, as well as his experience as a leader, McGregor began rethinking the conventions of modern management. He thought that the problem with corporate leadership wasn't so much its execution as its premises. Beginning with a speech in 1957, and later in a groundbreaking book called *The Human Side of Enterprise* in 1960, McGregor argued that those running companies were operating from faulty assumptions about human behavior.

Most leaders believed that the people in their organizations fundamentally disliked work and would avoid it if it they could. These faceless minions feared taking responsibility, craved security, and badly needed direction. As a result, "most people must be coerced, controlled, directed, and threatened with punishment to get them to put forth adequate effort toward the achievement of organizational objectives." But McGregor said there was an alternative view of employees—one that offered a more accurate assessment of the human condition and a more effective starting point for running companies. This perspective held that taking an interest in work is "as natural as play or rest," that creativity and ingenuity were widely distributed in the population, and that under the proper conditions, people will accept, and even seek, responsibility.[4]

To explain these contrasting outlooks, McGregor mined the back end of the alphabet. He called the first view Theory X and the second Theory Y. If your starting point was Theory X, he said, your managerial techniques would inevitably produce limited results, or even go awry entirely. If you believed in the "mediocrity of the masses," as he put it, then mediocrity became the ceiling on what you could achieve. But if your starting point was Theory Y, the possibilities were vast—not simply for the individual's potential, but for the company's bottom line as well. The way to make business organizations work better, therefore, was to shift management thinking away from Theory X and toward Theory Y.

Once again, the nomenclature stuck—and McGregor's approach

soon became a staple of management education.* A picture may be worth a thousand words—but sometimes neither is as potent as just two letters.

So with a hoist from Meyer Friedman onto the shoulders of Douglas McGregor, I'd like to introduce my own alphabetic way to think about human motivation.

TYPE I AND TYPE X

The Motivation 2.0 operating system depended on, and fostered, what I call Type X behavior. Type X behavior is fueled more by extrinsic desires than intrinsic ones. It concerns itself less with the inherent satisfaction of an activity and more with the external rewards to which that activity leads. The Motivation 3.0 operating system—the upgrade that's needed to meet the new realities of how we organize, think about, and do what we do—depends on what I call Type I behavior. Type I behavior is fueled more by intrinsic desires than extrinsic ones. It concerns itself less with the external rewards to which an activity leads and more with the inherent satisfaction of the activity itself. At the center of Type X behavior is the second drive. At the center of Type I behavior is the third drive.

If we want to strengthen our organizations, get beyond our decade of underachievement, and address the inchoate sense that something's gone wrong in our businesses, our lives, and our world, we need to move from Type X to Type I. (I use these two letters

*Alas, its impact was greater in the classroom than in the boardroom. Many companies did move their practices more in the direction of Theory Y. But talk to many managers even today and—in private—they'll often voice the same assumptions of Theory X that McGregor articulated in 1960.

largely to signify "extrinsic" and "intrinsic," but also to pay homage to Douglas McGregor.)

To be sure, reducing human behavior to two categories sacrifices a certain amount of nuance. And nobody exhibits purely Type X or Type I behavior every waking minute of every living day without exception. But we do have certain, often very clear, dispositions.

You probably know what I mean. Think about yourself. Does what energizes you—what gets you up in the morning and propels you through the day—come from the inside or from the outside? What about your spouse, your partner, or your children? How about the men and women around you at work? If you're like most people I've talked to, you instantly have a sense into which category someone belongs.*

I don't mean to say that Type X people always neglect the inherent enjoyment of what they do—or that Type I people resist outside goodies of any kind. But for Type X's, the main motivator is external rewards; any deeper satisfaction is welcome, but secondary. For Type I's, the main motivator is the freedom, challenge, and purpose of the undertaking itself; any other gains are welcome, but mainly as a bonus.

A few more distinctions to keep in mind before we go further:

Type I behavior is made, not born. These behavioral patterns aren't fixed traits. They are proclivities that emerge from circumstance, experience, and context. Type I behavior, because it arises in

---

*You can even try with this people you don't know. See if you agree. Enron's Jeff Skilling was Type X; Berkshire Hathaway's Warren Buffett is Type I. Antonio Salieri was Type X; Wolfgang Amadeus Mozart was Type I. The very wealthy Donald Trump is Type X; the even wealthier Oprah Winfrey is Type I. Former CEO of GE Jack Welch is Type X; Interface Global founder Ray Anderson is Type I. Simon Cowell is Type X; Bruce Springsteen is Type I. For a more nuanced view, check out the Type I Toolkit at the end of the book to find a free online assessment of the category to which you belong.

part from universal human needs, does not depend on age, gender, or nationality. The science demonstrates that once people learn the fundamental practices and attitudes—and can exercise them in supportive settings—their motivation, and their ultimate performance, soars. Any Type X can become a Type I.

Type I's almost always outperform Type X's in the long run. Intrinsically motivated people usually achieve more than their reward-seeking counterparts. Alas, that's not always true in the short term. An intense focus on extrinsic rewards can indeed deliver fast results. The trouble is, this approach is difficult to sustain. And it doesn't assist in mastery—which is the source of achievement over the long haul. The most successful people, the evidence shows, often aren't directly pursuing conventional notions of success. They're working hard and persisting through difficulties because of their internal desire to control their lives, learn about their world, and accomplish something that endures.

Type I behavior does not disdain money or recognition. Both Type X's and Type I's care about money. If an employee's compensation doesn't hit the baseline that I described in Chapter 2—if her organization doesn't pay her an adequate amount, or if her pay isn't equitable compared to others doing similar work—that person's motivation will crater, regardless of whether she leans toward X or toward I. However, once compensation meets that level, money plays a different role for Type I's than for Type X's. Type I's don't turn down raises or refuse to cash paychecks. But one reason fair and adequate pay is so essential is that it takes the issue of money off the table so they can focus on the work itself. By contrast, for many Type X's, money *is* the table. It's why they do what they do. Recognition is similar. Type I's like being recognized for their accomplishments—

because recognition is a form of feedback. But for them, unlike for Type X's, recognition is not a goal in itself.

Type I behavior is a renewable resource. Think of Type X behavior as coal and Type I behavior as the sun. For most of recent history, coal has been the cheapest, easiest, most efficient resource. But coal has two downsides. First, it produces nasty things like air pollution and greenhouse gases. Second, it's finite; getting more of it becomes increasingly difficult and expensive each year. Type X behavior is similar. An emphasis on rewards and punishments spews its own externalities (as enumerated in Chapter 2). And "if-then" motivators always grow more expensive. But Type I behavior, which is built around intrinsic motivation, draws on resources that are easily replenished and inflict little damage. It is the motivational equivalent of clean energy: inexpensive, safe to use, and endlessly renewable.

Type I behavior promotes greater physical and mental well-being. According to a raft of studies from SDT researchers, people oriented toward autonomy and intrinsic motivation have higher self-esteem, better interpersonal relationships, and greater general well-being than those who are extrinsically motivated. By contrast, people whose core aspirations are Type X validations such as money, fame, or beauty tend to have poorer psychological health. There's even a connection between Type X and Type A. Deci found that those oriented toward control and extrinsic rewards showed greater public self-consciousness, acted more defensively, and were more likely to exhibit the Type A behavior pattern.[5]

Ultimately, Type I behavior depends on three nutrients: autonomy, mastery, and purpose. Type I behavior is self-directed. It is devoted to becoming better and better at something that matters. And it connects that quest for excellence to a larger purpose.

Some might dismiss notions like these as gooey and idealistic, but the science says otherwise. The science confirms that this sort of behavior is essential to being human—and that now, in a rapidly changing economy, it is also critical for professional, personal, and organizational success of any kind.

So we have a choice. We can cling to a view of human motivation that is grounded more in old habits than in modern science. Or we can listen to the research, drag our business and personal practices into the twenty-first century, and craft a new operating system to help ourselves, our companies, and our world work a little better.

It won't be easy. It won't happen overnight. So let's get started.

Part Two

The Three Elements

CHAPTER 4

Autonomy

I've seen the future—and it works. It works in around-the-clock bursts in Sydney, Australia. It works on guerrilla-style side projects in Mountain View, California. And it works whenever it damn well pleases in Charlottesville, Virginia. The reason *why* it works is because of *how* it works. On the edges of the economy—slowly, but inexorably—old-fashioned ideas of management are giving way to a newfangled emphasis on self-direction.

That's why, a little past noon on a rainy Friday in Charlottesville, only a third of CEO Jeff Gunther's employees have shown up for work. But Gunther—entrepreneur, manager, capitalist—is neither worried nor annoyed. In fact, he's as calm and focused as a monk. Maybe that's because he didn't roll into the office himself until about an hour ago. Or maybe that's because he knows his crew isn't shirking. They're working—just on their own terms.

At the beginning of the year, Gunther launched an experiment in autonomy at Meddius, one of a trio of companies he runs. He turned the company, which creates computer software and hardware to help hospitals integrate their information systems, into a ROWE—a results-only work environment.

ROWEs are the brainchild of Cali Ressler and Jody Thompson, two former human resources executives at the American retailer Best Buy. ROWE's principles marry the commonsense pragmatism of Ben Franklin to the cage-rattling radicalism of Saul Alinsky. In a ROWE workplace, people don't have schedules. They show up when they want. They don't have to be in the office at a certain time—or any time, for that matter. They just have to get their work done. How they do it, when they do it, and where they do it is up to them.

That appealed to Gunther, who's in his early thirties. "Management isn't about walking around and seeing if people are in their offices," he told me. It's about creating conditions for people to do their best work. That's why he'd always tried to give employees a long leash. But as Meddius expanded, and as Gunther began exploring new office space, he started wondering whether talented, grown-up employees doing sophisticated work needed a leash of any length. So at the company's holiday dinner in December 2008, he made an announcement: For the first ninety days of the new year, the entire twenty-two-person operation would try an experiment. It would become a ROWE.

"In the beginning, people didn't take to it," Gunther says. The office filled up around nine A.M. and emptied out in the early evening, just as before. A few staffers had come out of extremely controlling environments and weren't accustomed to this kind of leeway. (At one employee's previous company, staff had to arrive each day by eight A.M. If someone was late, even by a few minutes, the employee had to write an explanation for everyone else to read.) But after a few weeks, most people found their groove. Productivity rose. Stress declined. And although two employees struggled with the freedom and left, by the end of the test period Gunther decided to go with ROWE permanently.

"Some people (outside of the company) thought I was crazy," he says. "They wondered, 'How can you know what your employees are doing if they're not here?'" But in his view, the team was accomplishing more under this new arrangement. One reason: They were focused on the work itself rather than on whether someone would call them a slacker for leaving at three P.M. to watch a daughter's soccer game. And since the bulk of his staff consists of software developers, designers, and others doing high-level creative work, that was essential. "For them, it's all about craftsmanship. And they need a lot of autonomy."

People still had specific goals they had to reach—for example, completing a project by a certain time or ringing up a particular number of sales. And if they needed help, Gunther was there to assist. But he decided against tying those goals to compensation. "That creates a culture that says it's all about the money and not enough about the work." Money, he believes, is only "a threshold motivator." People must be paid well and be able to take care of their families, he says. But once a company meets this baseline, dollars and cents don't much affect performance and motivation. Indeed, Gunther thinks that in a ROWE environment, employees are far less likely to jump to another job for a $10,000 or even $20,000 increase in salary. The freedom they have to do great work is more valuable, and harder to match, than a pay raise—and employees' spouses, partners, and families are among ROWE's staunchest advocates.

"More companies will migrate to this as more business owners my age come up. My dad's generation views human beings as human resources. They're the two-by-fours you need to build your house," he says. "For me, it's a partnership between me and the employees. They're not resources. They're partners." And partners, like all of us, need to direct their own lives.

PLAYERS OR PAWNS?

We forget sometimes that "management" does not emanate from nature. It's not like a tree or a river. It's like a television or a bicycle. It's something that humans invented. As the strategy guru Gary Hamel has observed, management is a technology. And like Motivation 2.0, it's a technology that has grown creaky. While some companies have oiled the gears a bit, and plenty more have paid lip service to the same, at its core management hasn't changed much in a hundred years. Its central ethic remains control; its chief tools remain extrinsic motivators. That leaves it largely out of sync with the nonroutine, right-brain abilities on which many of the world's economies now depend. But could its most glaring weakness run deeper? Is management, as it's currently constituted, out of sync with human nature itself?

The idea of management (that is, management of people rather than management of, say, supply chains) is built on certain assumptions about the basic natures of those being managed. It presumes that to take action or move forward, we need a prod—that absent a reward or punishment, we'd remain happily and inertly in place. It also presumes that once people do get moving, they need direction—that without a firm and reliable guide, they'd wander.

But is that really our fundamental nature? Or, to use yet another computer metaphor, is that our "default setting"? When we enter the world, are we wired to be passive and inert? Or are we wired to be active and engaged?

I'm convinced it's the latter—that our basic nature is to be curious and self-directed. And I say that not because I'm a dewy-eyed idealist, but because I've been around young children and because my wife and I have three kids of our own. Have you ever seen a six-month-old or a one-year-old who's *not* curious and self-directed? I haven't. That's how we are out of the box. If, at age fourteen or forty-three, we're passive and inert, that's not because it's our nature. It's because something flipped our default setting.

That something could well be management—not merely how bosses treat us at work, but also how the broader ethos has leeched into schools, families, and many other aspects of our lives. Perhaps management isn't *responding* to our supposedly natural state of passive inertia. Perhaps management is one of the forces that's switching our default setting and *producing* that state.

Now, that's not as insidious as it sounds. Submerging part of our nature in the name of economic survival can be a sensible move. My ancestors did it; so did yours. And there are times, even now, when we have no other choice.

But today economic accomplishment, not to mention personal fulfillment, more often swings on a different hinge. It depends not on keeping our nature submerged but on allowing it to surface. It requires resisting the temptation to control people—and instead doing everything we can to reawaken their deep-seated sense of autonomy. This innate capacity for self-direction is at the heart of Motivation 3.0 and Type I behavior.

The fundamentally autonomous quality of human nature is central to self-determination theory (SDT). As I explained in the previous chapter, Deci and Ryan cite autonomy as one of three basic human

> *"The ultimate freedom for creative groups is the freedom to experiment with new ideas. Some skeptics insist that innovation is expensive. In the long run, innovation is cheap. Mediocrity is expensive—and autonomy can be the antidote."*
>
> TOM KELLEY
> General Manager, IDEO

needs. And of the three, it's the most important—the sun around which SDT's planets orbit. In the 1980s, as they progressed in their work, Deci and Ryan moved away from categorizing behavior as either extrinsically motivated or intrinsically motivated to categorizing it as either controlled or autonomous. "Autonomous motivation involves behaving with a full sense of volition and choice," they write, "whereas controlled motivation involves behaving with the experience of pressure and demand toward specific outcomes that comes from forces perceived to be external to the self."[1]

Autonomy, as they see it, is different from independence. It's not the rugged, go-it-alone, rely-on-nobody individualism of the American cowboy. It means acting with choice—which means we can be both autonomous and happily interdependent with others. And while the idea of independence has national and political reverberations, autonomy appears to be a human concept rather than a western one. Researchers have found a link between autonomy and overall well-being not only in North America and Western Europe, but also in Russia, Turkey, and South Korea. Even in high-poverty non-Western locales like Bangladesh, social scientists have found that autonomy is something that people seek and that improves their lives.[2]

A sense of autonomy has a powerful effect on individual performance and attitude. According to a cluster of recent behavioral science studies, autonomous motivation promotes greater conceptual understanding, better grades, enhanced persistence at school and in sporting activities, higher productivity, less burnout, and greater levels of psychological well-being.[3] Those effects carry over to the workplace. In 2004, Deci and Ryan, along with Paul Baard of Fordham University, carried out a study of workers at an American investment bank. The three researchers found greater job satisfaction among employees whose bosses offered "autonomy support." These bosses saw issues from the employee's point of view, gave meaningful feedback and information, provided ample choice over what to do and how to do it, and encouraged employees to take on new projects. The resulting enhancement in job satisfaction, in turn, led to higher performance on the job. What's more, the benefits that autonomy confers on individuals extend to their organizations. For example, researchers at Cornell University studied 320 small businesses, half of which granted workers autonomy, the other half relying on top-down direction. The businesses that offered autonomy grew at four times the rate of the control-oriented firms and had one-third the turnover.[4]

Yet too many businesses remain woefully behind the science. Most twenty-first-century notions of management presume that, in the end, people are pawns rather than players. British economist Francis Green, to cite just one example, points to the lack of individual discretion at work as the main explanation for declining productivity and job satisfaction in the UK.[5] Management still revolves largely around supervision, "if-then" rewards, and other forms of control. That's true even of the kinder, gentler Motivation 2.1 approach that whispers sweetly about things like "empowerment" and "flexibility."

Indeed, just consider the very notion of "empowerment." It presumes that the organization has the power and benevolently ladles some of it into the waiting bowls of grateful employees. But that's not autonomy. That's just a slightly more civilized form of control. Or take management's embrace of "flex time." Ressler and Thompson call it a "con game," and they're right. Flexibility simply widens the fences and occasionally opens the gates. It, too, is little more than control in sheep's clothing. The words themselves reflect presumptions that run against both the texture of the times and the nature of the human condition. In short, management isn't the solution; it's the problem.

Perhaps it's time to toss the very word "management" onto the linguistic ash heap alongside "icebox" and "horseless carriage." This era doesn't call for better management. It calls for a renaissance of self-direction.

THE FOUR ESSENTIALS

In 2002, Scott Farquhar and Mike Cannon-Brookes, two wet-behind-the-ears Australians just out of university, borrowed $10,000 on their credit cards to start a software company. They anointed their venture with a bold name—Atlassian, after the Greek titan Atlas, who bore the world on his shoulders. And they set about creating a company to compete against some of the big names in enterprise software. At the time, their venture seemed loony. Today, it seems inspired. Through its combination of great computer code and smart business practices, Atlassian now rakes in about $35 million per year—and employs nearly two hundred people in offices in Sydney, Amsterdam, and San Francisco.

But like any good entrepreneur, Cannon-Brookes walks through life beneath a cloud of perpetual dissatisfaction. He'd seen successful companies stagnate and wished to avoid that fate for his. So to spark even greater creativity among his team, and to make sure Atlassian's programmers were having fun at work, he decided to encourage them to spend a day working on any problem they wanted, even if it wasn't part of their regular job.

This offbeat off-day gave birth to several ideas for new products and plenty of repairs and patches on existing ones. So Cannon-Brookes decided to make the practice a permanent part of the Atlassian culture. Now, once a quarter, the company sets aside an entire day when its engineers can work on any software problem they want—only this time, "to get them out of the day to day," it *must* be something that's not part of their regular job.

At two P.M. on a Thursday, the day begins. Engineers, including Cannon-Brookes himself, crash out new code or an elegant hack—any way they want, with anyone they want. Many work through the night. Then, at four P.M. on Friday, they show the results to the rest of the company in a wild-and-woolly all-hands meeting stocked with ample quantities of cold beer and chocolate cake. Atlassian calls these twenty-four-hour bursts of freedom and creativity "FedEx Days"—because people have to deliver something overnight. And deliver Atlassians have. Over the years, this odd little exercise has produced an array of software fixes that might otherwise never have emerged. Says one engineer, "Some of the coolest stuff we have in our product today has come from FedEx Days."

This isn't a pay-for-performance plan, grounded in the mechanistic assumptions of Motivation 2.0. It's an autonomy plan, nicely tuned to the alternate strains of Motivation 3.0. "We've always taken the position that money is only something you can lose on," Cannon-Brookes told me. "If you don't pay enough, you can lose people. But beyond that, money is not a motivator. What matters are these other features." And what a few future-facing businesses are discovering is that one of these essential features is autonomy—in particular, autonomy over four aspects of work: what people do, when they do it, how they do it, and whom they do it with. As Atlassian's experience shows, Type I behavior emerges when people have autonomy over the four T's: their *task*, their *time*, their *technique*, and their *team*.

Task

Cannon-Brookes was still dissatisfied. FedEx Days were working fine, but they had an inherent weakness. "You built something in twenty-four hours, but you didn't get any more time to work on it," he says. So he and cofounder Farquhar decided to double-down their bet on employee autonomy. In the spring of 2008, they announced that for the next six months, Atlassian developers could spend 20 percent of their time—rather than just one intense day—working on any project they wanted. As Cannon-Brookes explained in a blog post to employees:

> A startup engineer must be all things—he (or she) is a full time software developer and a part time product manager/ customer support guru/internal systems maven. As a company grows, an engineer spends less time building the things he personally wants in the product. Our hope is that 20% time gives engineers back dedicated stack time—of their own direction—to spend on product innovation, features, plugins, fixes or additions that they think are the most important.[6]

This practice has a sturdy tradition and a well-known modern expression. Its pioneer was the American company 3M. In the 1930s and 1940s, 3M's president and chairman was William McKnight, a fellow who was as unassuming in his manner as he was visionary in his thinking. McKnight believed in a simple, and at the time, subversive, credo: "Hire good people, and leave them alone." Well before it was fashionable for managers to flap on about "empowerment," he made a more vigorous case for autonomy. "Those men and women to whom we delegate authority and responsibility, if they are good people, are going to want to do their jobs in their own way," he wrote in 1948.[7] McKnight even encouraged employees to engage in what he called "experimental doodling."

> *"As an entrepreneur, I'm blessed with 100% autonomy over task, time, technique and team. Here's the thing: If I maintain that autonomy, I fail. I fail to ship. I fail to excel. I fail to focus. I inevitably end up either with no product or a product the market rejects. The art of the art is picking your limits. That's the autonomy I most cherish. The freedom to pick my boundaries."*
>
> SETH GODIN, Author of *Tribes,* *Purple Cow,* and the world's most popular marketing blog

With these unorthodox ideas percolating in his mind, this unlikely corporate heretic established a new policy: 3M's technical staff could spend up to 15 percent of their time on projects of their choosing. The initiative felt so counter to the mores of Motivation 2.0, so seemingly illicit, that inside the company, it was known as the "bootlegging policy." And yet it worked. These walled gardens of autonomy soon became fertile fields for a harvest of innovations—including Post-it notes. Scientist Art Fry came up with his idea for the ubiquitous stickie not in one of his regular assignments, but during his 15 percent time. Today, Post-its are a monumental business: 3M offers more than six hundred Post-it products in more than one hundred countries. (And their cultural impact might be even greater. Consider: But for McKnight's early push for autonomy, we'd be living in a world without any small yellow squares stuck to our computer monitors. A chilling thought indeed.) According to 3M's former head of research and development, most of the inventions that the company relies on even today emerged from those periods of bootlegging and experimental doodling.[8]

McKnight's innovation remains in place at 3M. But only a surprisingly small number of other companies have moved in this direction, despite its proven results. The best-known company to embrace it is Google, which has long encouraged engineers to spend one day a week working on a side project. Some Googlers use their "20 percent time" to fix an existing product, but most use it to develop something entirely new. Of course, Google doesn't sign away the intellectual property rights to what's created during that 20 percent—which is wise. In a typical year, more than half of Google's new offerings are birthed during this period of pure autonomy. For example, scientist Krishna Bharat, frustrated by how difficult it was to find news stories online, created Google News in his 20 percent time. The site now receives millions of visitors every day. Former Google engineer Paul Bucheit created Gmail, now one of the world's most popular e-mail programs, as his 20 percent project. Many other Google products share similar creation stories—among them Orkut (Google's social networking software), Google Talk (its instant message application), Google Sky (which allows astronomically inclined users to browse pictures of the universe), and Google Translate (its translation software for mobile devices). As Google engineer Alec Proudfoot, whose own 20 percent project aimed at boosting the efficiency of hybrid cars, put it in a television interview: "Just about all the good ideas here at Google have bubbled up from 20 percent time."[9]

Back at Atlassian, the experiment in 20 percent time seemed to work. In what turned out to be a yearlong trial, developers launched forty-eight new projects. So in 2009, Cannon-Brookes decided to make this dose of task autonomy a permanent feature of Atlassian work life. The decision didn't sit well with everyone. By Cannon-Brookes's back-of-the-blog calculations, seventy engineers, spending 20 percent of their time over just a six-month period, amounted to an investment of $1 million. The company's chief financial officer was aghast. Some project managers—despite Atlassian's forward-thinking ways, the company still uses the m-word—weren't happy, because it meant ceding some of their control over employees. When a few wanted to track employees' time to make sure they didn't abuse the privilege, Cannon-Brookes said no. "That was too controlling. I wanted to back our engineers and take it on faith that they'll do good things." Besides, he says, "People are way more efficient about 20 percent time than regular work time. They say, 'I'm not going to [expletive]ing do anything like read newsfeeds or do Facebook.'"

These days, when a finance guy, pearls of sweat rolling from his green eyeshades, objects to the price tag, Cannon-Brookes has a ready response: "I show him a long list of things we've delivered. I show him that we have zero turnover in engineering. And I show him that we have highly motivated engineers who are always trying to perfect and improve our product."

Autonomy over task is one of the essential aspects of the Motivation 3.0 approach to work. And it isn't reserved only for technology companies. At Georgetown University Hospital in Washington, D.C., for instance, many nurses have the freedom to conduct their own research projects, which in turn have changed a number of the hospital's programs and policies.[10] Autonomy measures can work in a range of fields—and offer a promising source for innovations and even institutional reforms.

Initiatives like FedEx Days and sanctioned side projects aren't always easy to execute in the day-to-day maw of serving customers, shipping products, and solving problems. But they're becoming urgent in an economy that demands nonroutine, creative, conceptual abilities—as any artist or designer would agree. Autonomy over task has long been critical to their ability to create. And good leaders (as opposed to competent "managers") understand this in their bones.

Case in point: George Nelson, who was the design director at Herman Miller, the iconic American furniture maker, for a few decades. He once laid down five simple tenets that he believed led to great design. One of these principles could serve as a rallying cry for Type I's ethic of autonomy over task: "You decide what you will make."

Time

Ever wonder why lawyers, as a group, are so miserable? Some social scientists have—and they've offered three explanations. One involves pessimism. Being pessimistic is almost always a recipe for low levels of what psychologists call "subjective well-being." It's also a detriment in most professions. But as Martin Seligman has written, "There is one glaring exception: pessimists do better at law." In other words, an attitude that makes someone less happy as a human being actually makes her more effective as a lawyer.[11] A second reason: Most other enterprises are positive-sum. If I sell you something you want and enjoy, we're both better off. Law, by contrast, is often (though not always) a zero-sum game: Because somebody wins, somebody else must lose.

But the third reason might offer the best explanation of all—and help us understand why so few attorneys exemplify Type I behavior. Lawyers often face intense demands but have relatively little "decision latitude." Behavioral scientists use this term to describe the choices, and perceived choices, a person has. In a sense, it's another way of describing autonomy—and lawyers are glum and cranky because they don't have much of it. The deprivation starts early. A 2007 study of two American law schools found that over the three-year period in school, students' overall well-being plummeted—in large part because their need for autonomy was thwarted. But students who had greater autonomy over their course selection, their assignments, and their relations with professors showed far less steep declines and actually posted better grades and bar exam scores.[12]

Alas, at the heart of private legal practice is perhaps the most autonomy-crushing mechanism imaginable: the billable hour. Most lawyers—and nearly all lawyers in large, prestigious firms—must keep scrupulous track, often in six-minute increments, of their time. If they fail to bill enough hours, their jobs are in jeopardy. As a result, their focus inevitably veers from the *output* of their work (solving a client's problem) to its *input* (piling up as many hours as possible). If the rewards come from time, then time is what firms will get. These sorts of high-stakes, measurable goals can drain intrinsic motivation, sap individual initiative, and even encourage unethical behavior. "If one is expected to bill more than two thousand hours per year," former U.S. Supreme Court Chief Justice William Rehnquist once said, "there are bound to be temptations to exaggerate the hours actually put in."[13]

The billable hour is a relic of Motivation 2.0. It makes some sense for routine tasks—whether fitting doors onto the body of a Ford Taurus or adding up deductions on a simple tax form—because there's a tight connection between how much time goes in and how much work comes out. And if your starting assumption is that workers' default setting is to shirk, monitoring their time can keep them on their toes.

But the billable hour has little place in Motivation 3.0. For nonroutine tasks, including law, the link between how much time

> "Nothing is more important to my success than controlling my schedule. I'm most creative from five to nine A.M. If I had a boss or co-workers, they would ruin my best hours one way or another."
>
> SCOTT ADAMS
> *Dilbert* creator

somebody spends and what that somebody produces is irregular and unpredictable. Imagine requiring inventor Dean Kamen or actress Helen Mirren to bill for their time. If we begin from an alternative, and more accurate, presumption—that people want to do good work—then we ought to let them focus on the work itself rather than the time it takes them to do it. Already, a few law firms are moving in this new, more Type I direction—charging a flat rate rather than a time-based fee—with the presiding partner of one of New York's leading law firms recently declaring, "This is the time to get rid of the billable hour."[14]

If the billable hour has an antithesis, it's the results-only work environment of the kind that Jeff Gunther has introduced at his companies. The first large company to go ROWE was Best Buy— not in its stores, but in its corporate offices. Like 3M's 15 percent time, Best Buy's ROWE experiment began as something of a rogue project launched by Ressler and Thompson, whom I mentioned earlier and who have since become ROWE gurus, taking their message of autonomy around the world. Best Buy's headquarters in Richfield, Minnesota, are airy, modern, and replete with a concierge, cafés, and dry cleaner. But the company had a reputation for punishing hours and intrusive bosses—and it was paying the price in lost talent. Best Buy's then CEO Brad Anderson quietly agreed to Ressler and Thompson's weird proposal, because it encouraged "people to contribute rather than just show up and grind out their days."[15]

Today, Best Buy's headquarters has fewer people working a regular schedule than it has those working a ROWE un-schedule. And even though retail electronics is a brutally competitive industry, Best Buy has held its own both in the marketplace and in its quest for talent. Reporting on the company's ROWE results in the *Harvard Business Review*, Tamara Erickson writes:

Salaried people put in as much time as it takes to do their work. Hourly employees in the program work a set number of hours to comply with federal labor regulations, but they get to choose when. Those employees report better relationships with family and friends, more company loyalty, and more focus and energy. Productivity has increased by 35%, and voluntary turnover is 320 basis points lower than in teams that have not made the change. Employees say they don't know whether they work fewer hours—they've stopped counting.[16]

Without sovereignty over our time, it's nearly impossible to have autonomy over our lives. A few Type I organizations have begun to recognize this truth about the human condition and to realign their practices. More, no doubt, will follow. "In the past, work was defined primarily by putting in time, and secondarily on getting results. We need to flip that model," Ressler told me. "No matter what kind of business you're in, it's time to throw away the tardy slips, time clocks, and outdated industrial-age thinking."

Technique

When you call a customer service line to complain about your cable television bill or to check the whereabouts of that blender you ordered, the phone usually rings in a colorless cavern known as a call center. The person who answers the call, a customer service representative, has a tough job. He typically sits for hours among a warren of cramped cubicles—headset strapped on, a diet soda by his side. The pay is paltry. And the people the rep encounters on the phone—one after another after another—generally aren't ringing up to offer kudos or to ask about the rep's weekend plans. They've got a gripe, a frustration, or a problem that needs solving. Right. Now.

If that weren't trying enough, call center reps have little decision latitude and their jobs are often the very definition of routine. When a call comes in, they listen to the caller—and then, in most cases, tap a few buttons on their computer to retrieve a script. Then they follow that script, sometimes word for word, in the hope of getting the caller off the line as quickly as possible. It can be deadening work, made drearier still because managers in many call centers, in an effort to boost productivity, listen in on reps' conversations and monitor how long each call lasts. Little wonder, then, that call centers in the United States and the UK have annual turnover rates that average about 35 percent, double the rate for other jobs. In some call centers the annual turnover rate exceeds 100 percent, meaning that, on average, none of the people working there today will be there a year from now.

Tony Hsieh, founder of the online shoe retailer Zappos.com (now part of Amazon.com), thought there was a better way to recruit, prepare, and challenge such employees. So new hires at Zappos go through a week of training. Then, at the end of those seven days, Hsieh makes them an offer. If they feel Zappos isn't for them and want to leave, he'll pay them $2,000—no hard feelings. Hsieh is hacking the Motivation 2.0 operating system like a brilliant and benevolent teenage computer whiz. He's using an "if-then" reward not to motivate people to perform better, but to weed out those who aren't fit for a Motivation 3.0–style workplace. The people who remain receive decent pay, and just as important, they have autonomy over technique. Zappos doesn't monitor its customer service employees' call times or require them to use scripts. The reps handle calls the way they want. Their job is to serve the customer well; how they do it is up to them.

The results of this emphasis on autonomy over technique? Turnover at Zappos is minimal. And although it's still young, Zappos consistently ranks as one of the best companies for customer service in the United States—ahead of better-known names like Cadillac, BMW, and Apple and roughly equal to ritzy brands like Jaguar and the Ritz-Carlton.[17] Not bad for a shoe company based in the Nevada desert.

What Zappos is doing is part of a small but growing move to restore some measure of individual freedom in jobs usually known for the lack of it. For instance, while many enterprises are offshoring work to low-cost providers overseas, some companies are reversing the trend by beginning what's known as "homeshoring." Instead of requiring customer service reps to report to a single large call center, they're routing the calls to the employees' homes. This cuts commuting time for staff, removes them from physical monitoring, and provides far greater autonomy over how they do their jobs.

The American airline JetBlue was one of the first to try this approach. From its launch in 2000, JetBlue has relied on telephone customer service employees who work at home. And from its launch, JetBlue has earned customer service rankings far ahead of its competitors. Productivity and job satisfaction are generally higher in homeshoring than in conventional arrangements—in part because employees are more comfortable and less monitored at home. But it's also because this autonomy-centered approach draws from a deeper pool of talent. Many homeshore employees are parents, students, retirees, and people with disabilities—those who want to work, but need to do it their own way. According to one report, between 70 and 80 percent of home-based customer service agents have college degrees—double the percentage among people working in traditional call centers. Ventures like Alpine Access, PHH Arval, and LiveOps, which run customer service departments for a range of companies, report that after adopting this method, their recruiting costs fall to almost zero.

Prospective employees come to them. And now these home-based customer service reps are working for a number of U.S. companies— including 1-800-Flowers, J. Crew, Office Depot, even the Internal Revenue Service—handling customer inquiries the way they choose.[18] As in any effective Motivation 3.0 workplace, it's their call.

Team .

Whatever your place in the birth order, consider what it's like to be the third child in a family. You don't get a say in choosing the people around you. They're there when you arrive. Worse, one or two of them might not be so glad to see you. And getting rid of even just one of them is usually impossible.

Taking a new job and holding most jobs are similar. Enterprising souls might be able to scratch out some autonomy over task, time, and technique—but autonomy over team is a taller order. That's one reason people are drawn to entrepreneurship— the chance to build a team of their own. But even in more traditional settings, although far from typical yet, a few organizations are discovering the virtues of offering people some amount of freedom over those with whom they work.

> "Autonomy over what we do is most important. The biggest difference between working for other studios and running my own has been the fact that I can choose what job we take on and what product, service, or institution we promote. This I find the single most important question: When I'm close to the content, research becomes easy, meetings become interesting (people who produce interesting products or services are mostly interesting themselves), and I don't have to be involved in false advertising."
>
> STEFAN SAGMEISTER
> Designer

For example, at the organic grocery chain Whole Foods, the people who are nominally in charge of each department don't do the hiring. That task falls to a department's employees. After a job candidate has worked a thirty-day trial period on a team, the prospective teammates vote on whether to hire that person full-time. At W. L. Gore & Associates, the makers of the GORE-TEX fabric and another example of Motivation 3.0 in action, anybody who wants to rise in the ranks and lead a team must assemble people willing to work with her.[19]

The ability to put together a pick-up basketball team of company talent is another attraction of 20 percent time. These initiatives usually slice across the organization chart, connecting people who share an interest, if not a department. As Google engineer Bharat Mediratta told *The New York Times*, "If your 20 percent idea is a new product, it's usually pretty easy to just find a few like-minded people and start coding away." And when pushing for a more systemic change in the organization, Mediratta says autonomy over team is even more important. Those efforts require what he calls a "grouplet"—a small, self-organized team that has almost no budget and even less authority, but that tries to change something within the company. For instance, Mediratta formed a testing grouplet to encourage engineers throughout the company to implement a more efficient way to test computer code. This informal band of coders, a team built autonomously without direction from the top, "slowly turned the organization on its axis."[20]

Still, the desire for autonomy can often collide with other obligations. One surprise as Atlassian ran the numbers on its task autonomy experiment was that most employees came in substantially under the 20 percent figure. The main reason? They didn't want to let down their current teammates by abandoning ongoing projects.

Although autonomy over team is the least developed of the four

T's, the ever-escalating power of social networks and the rise of mobile apps now make this brand of autonomy easier to achieve—and in ways that reach beyond a single organization. The open-source projects I mentioned in Chapter 1, in which ad hoc teams self-assemble to build a new browser or create better server software, are a potent example. And once again, the science affirms the value of something traditional businesses have been slow to embrace. Ample research has shown that people working in self-organized teams are more satisfied than those working in inherited teams.[21] Likewise, studies by Deci and others have shown that people high in intrinsic motivation are better coworkers.[22] And that makes the possibilities on this front enormous. If you want to work with more Type I's, the best strategy is to become one yourself. Autonomy, it turns out, can be contagious.

THE ART OF AUTONOMY

Think for a moment about the great artists of the last hundred years and how they worked—people like Pablo Picasso, Georgia O'Keeffe, and Jackson Pollock. Unlike for the rest of us, Motivation 2.0 was never their operating system. Nobody told them: *You must paint this sort of picture. You must begin painting precisely at eight-thirty A.M. You must paint with the people we select to work with you. And you must paint this way.* The very idea is ludicrous.

But you know what? It's ludicrous for you, too. Whether you're fixing sinks, ringing up groceries, selling cars, or writing a lesson plan, you and I need autonomy just as deeply as a great painter.

However, encouraging autonomy doesn't mean discouraging accountability. Whatever operating system is in place, people must be accountable for their work. But there are different ways to achieve this end, each built on different assumptions about who we are deep down. Motivation 2.0 assumed that if people had freedom, they would shirk—and that autonomy was a way to bypass accountability. Motivation 3.0 begins with a different assumption. It presumes that people *want* to be accountable—and that making sure they have control over their task, their time, their technique, and their team is a pathway to that destination.

Of course, because most workplaces still reverberate with the assumptions of the old operating system, transitioning to autonomy won't—often can't—happen in one fell swoop. If we pluck people out of controlling environments, when they've known nothing else, and plop them in a ROWE or an environment of undiluted autonomy, they'll struggle. Organizations must provide, as Richard Ryan puts it, "scaffolding" to help every employee find his footing to make the transition.

What's more, different individuals will prize different aspects of autonomy. Some might crave autonomy over a task; others might prefer autonomy over the team. As Zappos CEO Hsieh told me by e-mail, "Studies have shown that perceived control is an important component of one's happiness. However, what people feel like they want control over really varies, so I don't think there's one aspect of autonomy that's universally the most important. Different individuals have different desires, so the best strategy for an employer would be to figure out what's important to each individual employee."

Still, however those individual desires express themselves on the surface, they grow from common roots. We're born to be players, not pawns. We're meant to be autonomous individuals, not individual automatons. We're designed to be Type I. But outside forces—including the very idea that we need to be "managed"—have conspired to change our default setting and turn us into Type X. If we update the environments we're in—not only at work, but also at school and at home—and if leaders recognize both the truth of the human condition and the science that supports it, we can return ourselves and our colleagues to our natural state.

"The course of human history has always moved in the direction of greater freedom. And there's a reason for that—because it's in our nature to push for it," Ryan told me. "If we were just plastic like [some] people think, this wouldn't be happening. But somebody stands in front of a tank in China. Women, who've been denied autonomy, keep advocating for rights. This is the course of history. This is why ultimately human nature, if it ever realizes itself, will do so by becoming more autonomous."

CHAPTER 5

Mastery

You need not see what someone is doing
to know if it is his vocation,

you have only to watch his eyes:
a cook mixing a sauce, a surgeon

making a primary incision,
a clerk completing a bill of lading,

wear the same rapt expression, forgetting
themselves in a function.

How beautiful it is,
that eye-on-the-object look.

—*W. H. Auden*

One summer morning in 1944, Mihaly Csikszentmihalyi, age ten, stood on a train platform in Budapest, Hungary, with his mother, two brothers, and about seventy relatives who'd come to see them off. World War II was raging, and Hungary, an ambivalent member of the Axis, was being squeezed from every political and geographic corner. Nazi soldiers were occupying the country in retaliation for Hungary's secret peace negotiations with the United

States and Great Britain. Meanwhile, Soviet troops were advancing on the capital city.

It was time to leave. So the foursome boarded a train for Venice, Italy, where Csikszentmihalyi's father, a diplomat, was working. As the train rumbled southwest, bombs exploded in the distance. Bullets ripped through the train's windows, while a rifle-toting soldier on board fired back at the attackers. The ten-year-old crouched under his seat, terrified but also a little annoyed.

"It struck me at that point that grown-ups had really no idea how to live," Csikszentmihalyi told me some sixty-five years later.

His train would turn out to be the last to cross the Danube River for many years. Shortly after its departure, air strikes destroyed Hungary's major bridges. The Csikszentmihalyis were well educated and well connected, but the war flattened their lives. Of the relatives on the train platform that morning, more than half would be dead five months later. One of Csikszentmihalyi's brothers spent six years doing hard labor in the Ural Mountains. Another was killed fighting the Soviets.

"The whole experience got me thinking," Csikszentmihalyi said, recalling his ten-year-old self. "There has got to be a better way to live than this."

FROM COMPLIANCE TO ENGAGEMENT

The opposite of autonomy is control. And since they sit at different poles of the behavioral compass, they point us toward different destinations. Control leads to compliance; autonomy leads to engagement. And this distinction leads to the second element of Type I behavior: mastery—the desire to get better and better at something that matters.

As I explained in Part One, Motivation 2.0's goal was to encourage people to do particular things in particular ways—that is, to get them to comply. And for that objective, few motivators are more effective than a nice bunch of carrots and the threat of an occasional stick. This was rarely a promising route to self-actualization, of course. But as an economic strategy, it had a certain logic. For routine tasks, the sort of work that defined most of the twentieth century, gaining compliance usually worked just fine.

But that was then. For the definitional tasks of the twenty-first century, such a strategy falls short, often woefully short. Solving complex problems requires an inquiring mind and the willingness to experiment one's way to a fresh solution. Where Motivation 2.0 sought compliance, Motivation 3.0 seeks engagement. Only engagement can produce mastery. And the pursuit of mastery, an important but often dormant part of our third drive, has become essential in making one's way in today's economy.

Unfortunately, despite sweet-smelling words like "empowerment" that waft through corporate corridors, the modern workplace's most notable feature may be its lack of engagement and its disregard for mastery. Gallup's extensive research on the subject shows that in the United States, more than 50 percent of employees are not engaged at work—and nearly 20 percent are actively disengaged. The cost of all this disengagement: about $300 billion a year in lost productivity—a sum larger than the GDP of Portugal, Singapore, or Israel.[1] Yet in comparative terms, the United States looks like a veritable haven of Type I behavior at work. According to the consulting firm McKinsey & Co., in some countries as little as 2 to 3 percent of the workforce is highly engaged in their work.[2]

Equally important, engagement as a route to mastery is a powerful force in our personal lives. While complying can be an effective strategy for physical survival, it's a lousy one for personal fulfillment. Living a satisfying life requires more than simply meeting the demands of those in control. Yet in our offices and our classrooms we have way too much compliance and way too little engagement. The former might get you through the day, but only the latter will get you through the night. And that brings us back to Csikszentmihalyi's story.

In his early teens, after witnessing the atrocities of Nazi Germany and the Soviet takeover of his country, Csikszentmihalyi was understandably weary of compliance and looking for engagement. But he wouldn't find it at school. He dropped out of high school at thirteen. For nearly a decade, he worked in various Western European countries at a series of jobs, some odder than others, to support himself. And hoping to answer his youthful question about a better way to live, he read everything he could get his hands on in religion and philosophy. What he learned didn't satisfy him. It wasn't until he inadvertently stumbled into a lecture by none other than Carl Jung that he heard about the field of psychology and decided that it might hold the secrets he sought.

So in 1956, at the age of twenty-two, Csikszentmihalyi set off for the United States to study psychology. He arrived in Chicago, a high school dropout with $1.25 in his pocket whose only familiarity with the English language came from reading *Pogo* comic strips. Hungarian contacts in Chicago helped him find a job and a place to live. His knowledge of Latin, German, and *Pogo* helped him pass the Illinois high school equivalency test in a language he neither spoke nor read. He enrolled in the University of Illinois–Chicago, took classes during the day, worked as a hotel auditor at night, and eventually wound up at the University of Chicago psychology department, where—just nine years after setting foot in America—he earned a Ph.D.

But Csikszentmihalyi resisted rafting down the main currents of his field. As he told me one spring morning not long ago, he wanted to explore "the positive, innovative, creative approach to life instead of the remedial, pathological view that Sigmund Freud had or the mechanistic work" of B. F. Skinner and others who reduced behavior to simple stimulus and response. He began by writing about creativity. Creativity took him into the study of play. And his exploration of play unlocked an insight about the human experience that would make him famous.

In the midst of play, many people enjoyed what Csikszentmihalyi called "autotelic experiences"—from the Greek *auto* (self) and *telos* (goal or purpose). In an autotelic experience, the goal is self-fulfilling; the activity is its own reward. Painters he observed during his Ph.D. research, Csikszentmihalyi said, were so enthralled in what they were doing that they seemed to be in a trance. For them, time passed quickly and self-consciousness dissolved. He sought out other people who gravitated to these sorts of pursuits—rock climbers, soccer players, swimmers, spelunkers—and interviewed them to discover what made an activity autotelic. It was frustrating. "When people try to recall how it felt to climb a mountain or play a great musical piece," Csikszentmihalyi later wrote, "their stories are usually quite stereotyped and uninsightful."[3] He needed a way to probe people's experiences in the moment. And in the mid-1970s, a bold new technology—one that any twelve-year-old now would find laughingly retrograde—came to the rescue: the electronic pager.

Csikszentmihalyi, who by then was teaching at the University of

Chicago and running his own psychology lab, clipped on a pager and asked his graduate students to beep him randomly several times each day. Whenever the pager sounded, he recorded what he was doing and how he was feeling. "It was so much fun," he recalled in his office at the Claremont Graduate University in southern California, where he now teaches. "You got such a detailed picture of how people lived." On the basis of this test run, he developed a methodology called the Experience Sampling Method. Csikszentmihalyi would page people eight times a day at random intervals and ask them to write in a booklet their answers to several short questions about what they were doing, who they were with, and how they'd describe their state of mind. Put the findings together for seven days and you had a flip book, a mini-movie, of someone's week. Assemble the individual findings and you had an entire library of human experiences.

From these results, Csikszentmihalyi began to peel back the layers of those autotelic experiences. Perhaps equally significant, he replaced that wonky Greek-derived adjective with a word he found people using to describe these optimal moments: flow. The highest, most satisfying experiences in people's lives were when they were in flow. And this previously unacknowledged mental state, which seemed so inscrutable and transcendent, was actually fairly easy to unpack. In flow, goals are clear. You have to reach the top of the mountain, hit the ball across the net, or mold the clay just right. Feedback is immediate. The mountaintop gets closer or farther, the ball sails in or out of bounds, the pot you're throwing comes out smooth or uneven.

Most important, in flow, the relationship between what a person had to do and what he could do was perfect. The challenge wasn't too easy. Nor was it too difficult. It was a notch or two beyond his current abilities, which stretched the body and mind in a way that made the effort itself the most delicious reward. That balance produced a degree of focus and satisfaction that easily surpassed other, more quotidian, experiences. In flow, people lived so deeply in the moment, and felt so utterly in control, that their sense of time, place, and even self melted away. They were autonomous, of course. But more than that, they were engaged. They were, as the poet W. H. Auden wrote, "forgetting themselves in a function."

Maybe this state of mind was what that ten-year-old boy was seeking as that train rolled through Europe. Maybe reaching flow, not for a single moment but as an ethic for living—maintaining that beautiful "eye-on-the-object look" to achieve mastery as a cook, a surgeon, or a clerk—was the answer. Maybe this was the way to live.

GOLDILOCKS ON A CARGO SHIP

Several years ago—he can't recall exactly when—Csikszentmihalyi was invited to Davos, Switzerland, by Klaus Schwab, who runs an annual conclave of the global power elite in that city.

> *"The desire to do something because you find it deeply satisfying and personally challenging inspires the highest levels of creativity, whether it's in the arts, sciences, or business."*
>
> TERESA AMABILE
> Professor, Harvard University

Joining him on the trip were three other University of Chicago faculty members—Gary Becker, George Stigler, and Milton Friedman—all of them economists, all of them winners of the Nobel Prize. The five men gathered for dinner one night and at the end of the meal, Schwab asked the academics what they considered the most important issue in modern economics.

"To my incredulous surprise," Csikszentmihalyi recounted, "Becker, Stigler, and Friedman all ended up saying a variation of 'There's something missing,'" that for all its explanatory power, economics still failed to offer a rich enough account of behavior, even in business settings.

Csikszentmihalyi smiled and complimented his colleagues on their perspicacity. The concept of flow, which he introduced in the mid-1970s, was not an immediate game-changer. It gained some traction in 1990 when Csikszentmihalyi wrote his first book on the topic for a wide audience and gained a small band of followers in the business world. However, putting this notion into place in the real operations of real organizations has been slower going. After all, Motivation 2.0 has little room for a concept like flow. The Type X operating system doesn't oppose people taking on optimal challenges on the job, but it suggests that such moments are happy accidents rather than necessary conditions for people to do great work.

But ever so slowly the ground might be shifting. As the data on worker disengagement earlier in the chapter reveal, the costs—in both human satisfaction and organizational health—are high when a workplace is a no-flow zone. That's why a few enterprises are trying to do things differently. As *Fast Company* magazine has noted, a number of companies, including Microsoft, Patagonia, and Toyota, have realized that creating flow-friendly environments that help people move toward mastery can increase productivity and satisfaction at work.[4]

For example, Stefan Falk, a vice president at Ericsson, the Swedish telecommunications concern, used the principles of flow to smooth a merger of the company's business units. He persuaded managers to configure work assignments so that employees had clear objectives and a way to get quick feedback. And instead of meeting with their charges for once-a-year performance reviews, managers sat down with employees one-on-one six times a year, often for as long as ninety minutes, to discuss their level of engagement and path toward mastery. The flow-centered strategy worked well enough that Ericsson began using it in offices around the world. After that, Falk moved to Green Cargo, an enormous logistics and shipping company in Sweden. There, he developed a method of training managers in how flow worked. Then he required them to meet with staff once a month to get a sense of whether people were overwhelmed or underwhelmed with their work—and to adjust assignments to help them find flow. After two years of managerial revamping, state-owned Green Cargo became profitable for the first time in 125 years—and executives cite its newfound flowcentricity as a key reason.[5]

In addition, a study of 11,000 industrial scientists and engineers working at companies in the United States found that the desire for intellectual challenge—that is, the urge to master something new and engaging—was the best predictor of productivity. Scientists motivated by this intrinsic desire filed significantly more patents than those whose main motivation was money, even controlling for the amount of effort each group expended.[6] (That is, the extrinsically motivated group worked as long and as hard as their more Type I colleagues. They just accomplished less—perhaps because they spent less of their work time in flow.)

And then there's Jenova Chen, a young game designer who, in 2006, wrote his MFA thesis on Csikszentmihalyi's theory. Chen believed that video games held the promise to deliver quintessential flow experiences, but that too many games required an almost obsessive level of commitment. Why not, he thought, design a game to bring the flow sensation to more casual gamers? Using his thesis project as his laboratory, Chen created a game in which players use a computer mouse to guide an on-screen amoeba-like organism through a surreal ocean landscape as it gobbles other creatures and slowly evolves into a higher form. While most games require players to proceed through a fixed and predetermined series of skill levels, Chen's allows them to advance and explore any way they desire. And unlike games in which failure ends the session, in Chen's game failure merely pushes the player to a level better matched to her ability. Chen calls his game flOw. And it's been a huge hit. People have played the free online version of the game more than three million times. (You can find it at http://intihuatani.usc.edu/cloud/flowing/). The paid version, designed for the PlayStation game console, has generated more than 350,000 downloads and collected a shelf full of awards. Chen used the game to launch his own firm, thatgamecompany, built around both flow and flOw, that quickly won a three-game development deal from Sony, something almost unheard of for an unknown start-up run by a couple of twenty-six-year-old California game designers.

Green Cargo, thatgamecompany, and the companies employing the patent-cranking scientists typically use two tactics that their less savvy competitors do not. First, they provide employees with what I call "Goldilocks tasks"—challenges that are not too hot and not too cold, neither overly difficult nor overly simple. One source of frustration in the workplace is the frequent mismatch between what people *must* do and what people *can* do. When what they must do exceeds their capabilities, the result is anxiety. When what they must do falls short of their capabilities, the result is boredom. (Indeed, Csikszentmihalyi titled his first book on autotelic experiences *Beyond Boredom and Anxiety*.) But when the match is just right, the results can be glorious. This is the essence of flow. Goldilocks tasks offer us the powerful experience of inhabiting the zone, of living on the knife's edge between order and disorder, of—as painter Fritz Scholder once described it—"walking the tightrope between accident and discipline."

The second tactic that smart organizations use to increase their flow-friendliness and their employees' opportunities for mastery is to trigger the positive side of the Sawyer Effect. Recall from Chapter 2 that extrinsic rewards can turn play into work. But it's also possible to run the current in the other direction—and turn work into play. Some tasks at work don't automatically provide surges of flow, yet still need to get done. So the shrewdest enterprises afford employees the freedom to sculpt their jobs in ways that bring a little bit of flow to otherwise mundane duties. Amy Wrzesniewski and Jane Dutton, two business school professors, have studied this phenomenon among hospital cleaners, nurses, and hairdressers. They found, for instance, that some members of the cleaning staff at hospitals, instead of doing the minimum the job required, took on new tasks—from chatting with patients to helping make nurses' jobs go more smoothly. Adding these more absorbing challenges increased these cleaners' satisfaction and boosted their own views of their skills. By reframing aspects of their duties, they helped make work more playful and more fully their own. "Even in low-autonomy jobs," Wrzesniewski and Dutton write, "employees can create new domains for mastery."[7]

THE THREE LAWS OF MASTERY

Flow is essential to mastery. But flow doesn't guarantee mastery—because the two concepts operate on different horizons of time. One happens in a moment; the other unfolds over months, years, sometimes decades. You and I each might reach flow tomorrow morning—but neither one of us will achieve mastery overnight.

So how can we enlist flow in the quest for something that goes deeper and endures longer? What can we do to move toward mastery, one of the key elements of Type I behavior, in our organizations and our lives? A few behavioral scientists have offered some initial answers to those questions, and their findings suggest that mastery abides by three, somewhat peculiar, laws.

Mastery Is a Mindset

As with so many things in life, the pursuit of mastery is all in our head. At least that's what Carol Dweck has discovered.

Dweck, a psychology professor at Stanford University, has been studying motivation and achievement in children and young adults for nearly forty years, amassing a body of rigorous empirical research that has made her a superstar in contemporary behavioral science. Dweck's signature insight is that what people believe shapes what people achieve. Our beliefs about ourselves and the nature of our abilities—what she calls our "self-theories"—determine how we interpret our experiences and can set the boundaries on what we accomplish. Although her research looks mostly at notions of "intelligence," her findings apply with equal force to most human capabilities. And they yield the first law of mastery: *Mastery is a mindset*.

According to Dweck, people can hold two different views of their own intelligence. Those who have an

> *"Figure out for yourself what you want to be really good at, know that you'll never really satisfy yourself that you've made it, and accept that that's okay."*
>
> ROBERT B. REICH
> Former U.S. Secretary of Labor

"entity theory" believe that intelligence is just that—an entity. It exists within us, in a finite supply that we cannot increase. Those who subscribe to an "incremental theory" take a different view. They believe that while intelligence may vary slightly from person to person, it is ultimately something that, with effort, we can increase. To analogize to physical qualities, incremental theorists consider intelligence as something like strength. (Want to get stronger and more muscular? Start pumping iron.) Entity theorists view it as something more like height. (Want to get taller? You're out of luck.)* If you believe intelligence is a fixed quantity, then every educational and professional encounter becomes a measure of how much you have. If you believe intelligence is something you can increase, then the same encounters become opportunities for growth. In one view, intelligence is something you demonstrate; in the other, it's something you develop.

The two self-theories lead down two very different paths—one that heads toward mastery and one that doesn't. For instance, consider goals. Dweck says they come in two varieties—performance goals and learning goals. Getting an A in French class is a performance

---

*In her 2006 book, *Mindset: The New Psychology of Success*, which I recommend in the Type I Toolkit, Dweck refers to these two views as the "fixed mindset" and the "growth mindset."

goal. Being able to speak French is a learning goal. "Both goals are entirely normal and pretty much universal," Dweck says, "and both can fuel achievement."[8] But only one leads to mastery. In several studies, Dweck found that giving children a performance goal (say, getting a high mark on a test) was effective for relatively straight-forward problems but often inhibited children's ability to apply the concepts to new situations. For example, in one study, Dweck and a colleague asked junior high students to learn a set of scientific principles, giving half of the students a performance goal and half a learning goal. After both groups demonstrated they had grasped the material, researchers asked the students to apply their knowledge to a new set of problems, related but not identical to what they'd just studied. Students with learning goals scored significantly higher on these novel challenges. They also worked longer and tried more solutions. As Dweck writes, "With a learning goal, students don't have to feel that they're already good at something in order to hang in and keep trying. After all, their goal is to learn, not to prove they're smart."[9]

Indeed, the two self-theories take very different views of effort. To incremental theorists, exertion is positive. Since incremental theorists believe that ability is malleable, they see working harder as a way to get better. By contrast, says Dweck, "the entity theory . . . is a system that requires a diet of easy successes." In this schema, if you have to work hard, it means you're not very good. People therefore choose easy targets that, when hit, affirm their existing abilities but do little to expand them. In a sense, entity theorists want to look like masters without expending the effort to attain mastery.

Finally, the two types of thinking trigger contrasting responses to adversity—one that Dweck calls "helpless," the other, "mastery-oriented." In a study of American fifth- and sixth-graders, Dweck gave students eight conceptual problems they could solve, followed by four they could not (because the questions were too advanced for children that age). Students who subscribed to the idea that brainpower is fixed gave up quickly on the tough problems and blamed their (lack of) intelligence for their difficulties. Students with a more expansive mindset kept working in spite of the difficulty and deployed far more inventive strategies to find a solution. What did these students blame for their inability to conquer the toughest problems? "The answer, which surprised us, was that they didn't blame anything," Dweck says. The young people recognized that setbacks were inevitable on the road to mastery and that they could even be guideposts for the journey.

Dweck's insights map nicely to the behavioral distinctions underlying Motivation 2.0 and Motivation 3.0. Type X behavior often holds an entity theory of intelligence, prefers performance goals to learning goals, and disdains effort as a sign of weakness. Type I behavior has an incremental theory of intelligence, prizes learning goals over performance goals, and welcomes effort as a way to improve at something that matters. Begin with one mindset, and mastery is impossible. Begin with the other, and it can be inevitable.

Mastery Is a Pain

Each summer, about twelve hundred young American men and women arrive at the United States Military Academy at West Point to begin four years of study and to take their place in the fabled "long gray line." But before any of them sees a classroom, they go through seven weeks of Cadet Basic Training—otherwise known

> *"Try to pick a profession in which you enjoy even the most mundane, tedious parts. Then you will always be happy."*
>
> WILL SHORTZ
> Puzzle guru

as "Beast Barracks." By the time the summer ends, one in twenty of these talented, dedicated young adults has dropped out. A group of scholars—two from West Point, another from the University of Pennsylvania, and a fourth from the University of Michigan—wanted to understand why some students continued on the road toward military mastery and others got off at the first exit.

Was it physical strength and athleticism? Intellect? Leadership ability? Well-roundedness?

None of the above. The best predictor of success, the researchers found, was the prospective cadets' ratings on a noncognitive, non-physical trait known as "grit"—defined as "perseverance and passion for long-term goals."[10] The experience of these army officers-in-training confirms the second law of mastery: *Mastery is a pain.*

As wonderful as flow is, the path to mastery—becoming ever better at something you care about—is not lined with daisies and spanned by a rainbow. If it were, more of us would make the trip. Mastery hurts. Sometimes—many times—it's not much fun. That is one lesson of the work of psychologist Anders Ericsson, whose groundbreaking research on expert performance has provided a new theory of what fosters mastery. As he puts it, "Many characteristics once believed to reflect innate talent are actually the results of intense practice for a minimum of 10 years."[11] Mastery—of sports, music, business—requires effort (difficult, painful, excruciating, all-consuming effort) over a long time (not a week or a month, but a decade).[12] Sociologist Daniel Chambliss has referred to this as "the mundanity of excellence." Like Ericsson, Chambliss found—in a three-year study of Olympic swimmers—that those who did the best typically spent the most time and effort on the mundane activities that readied them for races.[13] It's the same reason that, in another study, the West Point grit researchers found that grittiness—rather than IQ or standardized test scores—is the most accurate predictor of college grades. As they explained, "Whereas the importance of working harder is easily apprehended, the importance of working longer without switching objectives may be less perceptible . . . in every field, grit may be as essential as talent to high accomplishment."[14]

Flow enters the picture here in two ways. If people are conscious of what puts them in flow, they'll have a clearer idea of what they should devote the time and dedication to master. And those moments of flow in the course of pursuing excellence can help people through the rough parts. But in the end, mastery often involves working and working and showing little improvement, perhaps with a few moments of flow pulling you along, then making a little progress, and then working and working on that new, slightly higher plateau again. It's grueling, to be sure. But that's not the problem; that's the solution.

As Carol Dweck says, "Effort is one of the things that gives meaning to life. Effort means you care about something, that something is important to you and you are willing to work for it. It would be an impoverished existence if you were not willing to value things and commit yourself to working toward them."[15]

Another doctor, one who lacks a Ph.D. but has a plaque in the Basketball Hall of Fame in Springfield, Massachusetts, put it similarly. "Being a professional," Julius Erving once said, "is doing the things you love to do, on the days you don't feel like doing them."[16]

Mastery Is an Asymptote

To understand the final law of mastery, you need to know a little algebra and a little art history.

From algebra, you might remember the concept of an asymptote. If not, maybe you'll recognize it below. An asymptote (in this case, a horizontal asymptote) is a straight line that a curve approaches but never quite reaches.

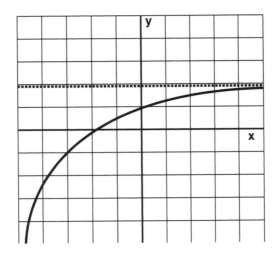

From art history, you might remember Paul Cézanne, the nineteenth-century French painter. You needn't remember much—just that he was significant enough to have art critics and scholars write about him. Cézanne's most enduring paintings came late in his life. And one reason for this, according to University of Chicago economist David Galenson, who's studied the careers of artists, is that he was endlessly trying to realize his best work. For Cézanne, one critic wrote, the ultimate synthesis of a design was never revealed in a flash; rather he approached it with infinite precautions, stalking it, as it were, now from one point of view, now from another. . . . *For him the synthesis was an asymptote toward which he was for ever approaching without ever quite reaching it.*[17]

This is the nature of mastery: *Mastery is an asymptote.*

You can approach it. You can home in on it. You can get really, really, really close to it. But like Cézanne, you can *never* touch it. Mastery is impossible to realize fully. Tiger Woods, perhaps the greatest golfer of all time, has said flatly that he can—that he must—become better. He said it when he was an amateur. He'll say it after his best outing or at the end of his finest season. He's pursuing mastery. That's well-known. What's less well-known is that he understands that he'll never get it. It will always hover beyond his grasp.

The mastery asymptote is a source of frustration. Why reach for something you can never fully attain? But it's also a source of allure. Why *not* reach for it? The joy is in the pursuit more than the realization. In the end, mastery attracts precisely because mastery eludes.

THE OXYGEN OF THE SOUL

The subjects were displaying the warning signs of "generalized anxiety disorder," a mental illness that afflicts roughly 3 percent of the adult population. According to the *Diagnostic and Statistical Manual of Mental Disorders* (*DSM-IV*), the presence of any three of the following six symptoms indicates what could be a serious problem:

- Restlessness or feeling keyed up or on edge
- Being easily fatigued
- Difficulty concentrating or mind going blank
- Irritability
- Muscle tension
- Sleep disturbance

These men and women seemed textbook cases. One person, who had previously glided through life with equanimity, now felt "tense, more hostile, angry, and irritated." Another reported being "more irritable, restless," and suffering from "shorter concentration." Yet another scribbled this self-description: "Slept badly, listless, more nervous, more guarded." Some people feared they were having a nervous breakdown. One person's mind was so muddied that he inadvertently walked into a wall and broke his glasses.

Time for a trip to the psychiatrist or a prescription for antianxiety medicine?

No. It was time for people to let flow back into their lives. In the early 1970s, Csikszentmihalyi conducted an experiment in which he asked people to record all the things they did in their lives that were "noninstrumental"—that is, small activities they undertook not out of obligation or to achieve a particular objective, but because they enjoyed them. Then he issued the following set of instructions:

Beginning [morning of target date], when you wake up and until 9:00 PM, we would like you to act in a normal way, doing all the things you have to do, but not doing anything that is "play" or "noninstrumental."

In other words, he and his research team directed participants to scrub their lives of flow. People who liked aspects of their work had to avoid situations that might trigger enjoyment. People who relished demanding physical exercise had to remain sedentary. One woman enjoyed washing dishes because it gave her something constructive to do, along with time to fantasize free of guilt, but could wash dishes only when absolutely necessary.

The results were almost immediate. Even at the end of the first day, participants "noticed an increased sluggishness about their behavior." They began complaining of headaches. Most reported difficulty concentrating, with "thoughts [that] wander round in circles without getting anywhere." Some felt sleepy, while others were too agitated to sleep. As Csikszentmihalyi wrote, "After just two days of deprivation . . . the general deterioration in mood was so advanced that prolonging the experiment would have been unadvisable."[18]

Two days. Forty-eight hours without flow plunged people into a state eerily similar to a serious psychiatric disorder. The experiment suggests that flow, the deep sense of engagement that Motivation 3.0 calls for, isn't a nicety. It's a necessity. We need it to survive. It is the oxygen of the soul.

And one of Csikszentmihalyi's more surprising findings is that people are much more likely to reach that flow state at work than in leisure. Work can often have the structure of other autotelic experiences: clear goals, immediate feedback, challenges well matched to our abilities. And when it does, we don't just enjoy it more, we do it better. That's why it's so odd that organizations tolerate work environments that deprive large numbers of people of these experiences. By offering a few more Goldilocks tasks, by looking for ways to unleash the positive side of the Sawyer Effect, organizations can help their own cause and enrich people's lives.

Csikszentmihalyi grasped this essential reality more than thirty years ago, when he wrote, "There is no reason to believe any longer that only irrelevant 'play' can be enjoyed, while the serious business of life must be borne as a burdensome cross. Once we realize that the boundaries between work and play are artificial, we can take matters in hand and begin the difficult task of making life more livable."[19]

But if we're looking for guidance on how to do this right—on how to make mastery an ethic for living—our best role models are probably not sitting around a boardroom table or working in the office down the hall.

Over lunch, Csikszentmihalyi and I talked about children. A little kid's life bursts with autotelic experiences. Children career from one flow moment to another, animated by a sense of joy, equipped with a mindset of possibility, and working with the dedication of a West Point cadet. They use their brains and their bodies to probe and draw feedback from the environment in an endless pursuit of mastery.

Then—at some point in their lives—they don't. What happens?

"You start to get ashamed that what you're doing is childish," Csikszentmihalyi explained.

What a mistake. Perhaps you and I—and all the other adults in charge of things—are the ones who are immature. It goes back to Csikszentmihalyi's experience on the train, wondering how grown-ups could have gotten things so wrong. Our circumstances may be less dire, but the observation is no less acute. Left to their own devices, Csikszentmihalyi says, children seek out flow with the inevitability of a natural law. So should we all.

CHAPTER 6

Purpose

We know from statisticians that demographics is destiny. And we know from the Rolling Stones that you can't always get what you want. What we don't know is what happens when these two indomitable principles sit down, pour themselves a drink, and get to know each other better.

But we're about to find out.

In 2006, the first members of the baby-boom generation began turning sixty. On birthdays with big round numbers, people usually stop, reflect, and take stock of their lives. And I've found that when boomers, in the United States and elsewhere, reach this milestone, they typically move through a three-stage reaction.

In the first stage, they ask: "How the heck did I get to be sixty?" When their odometer flips to 6-0, people often are surprised and slightly alarmed. Sixty, they think, is old. They tally their regrets and confront the reality that Mick Jagger and crew were right, that they didn't always get what they wanted.

But then the second stage kicks in. In the not-so-distant past, turning sixty meant that you were somewhat, ahem, long in the tooth. But at the beginning of the twenty-first century, anyone who's healthy enough to have made it six decades is probably healthy enough to hang on a fair bit longer. According to United Nations data, a sixty-year-old American man can expect to live for another twenty-plus years; a sixty-year-old American woman will be around for another quarter of a century. In Japan, a sixty-year-old man can expect to live past his eighty-second birthday, a sixty-year-old woman to nearly eighty-eight. The pattern is the same in many other prosperous countries. In France, Israel, Italy, Switzerland, Canada, and elsewhere, if you've reached the age of sixty, you're more than likely to live into your eighties.[1] And this realization brings with it a certain relief. "Whew," the boomer in Toronto or Osaka sighs. "I've got a couple more decades."

But the relief quickly dissipates—because almost as soon as the sigh fades, people enter the third stage. Upon comprehending that they could have another twenty-five years, sixty-year-old boomers look *back* twenty-five years—to when they were thirty-five—and a sudden thought clonks them on the side of the head. "Wow. That sure happened fast," they say. "Will the next twenty-five years race by like that? If so, when am I going to do something that matters? When am I going to live my best life? When am I going to make a difference in the world?"

Those questions, which swirl through conversations taking place at boomer kitchen tables around the world, may sound touchy-feely. But they're now occurring at a rate that is unprecedented in human civilization. Consider: Boomers are the largest demographic cohort in most western countries, as well as in places like Japan, Australia, and New Zealand. According to the U.S. Census Bureau, the United States alone has about 78 million boomers—which means that, on average, each year more than four million Americans hit this soul-searching, life-pondering birthday.[2] That's more than 11,000 people each day, more than 450 every hour.

In other words, in America alone, one hundred boomers turn sixty every thirteen minutes.

Every thirteen minutes another hundred people—members of the wealthiest and best-educated generation the world has ever known—begin reckoning with their mortality and asking deep questions about meaning, significance, and what they truly want.

One hundred people. Every thirteen minutes. Every hour. Of every day. Until 2024.

When the cold front of demographics meets the warm front of unrealized dreams, the result will be a thunderstorm of purpose the likes of which the world has never seen.

THE PURPOSE MOTIVE

The first two legs of the Type I tripod, autonomy and mastery, are essential. But for proper balance we need a third leg—purpose, which provides a context for its two mates. Autonomous people working toward mastery perform at very high levels. But those who do so in the service of some greater objective can achieve even more. The most deeply motivated people—not to mention those who are most productive and satisfied—hitch their desires to a cause larger than themselves.

Motivation 2.0, however, doesn't recognize purpose as a motivator. The Type X operating system doesn't banish the concept, but it

> *"I believe wholeheartedly that a new form of capitalism is emerging. More stakeholders (customers, employees, shareholders, and the larger community) want their businesses to . . . have a purpose bigger than their product."*
>
> MATS LEDERHAUSEN
> Investor and former
> McDonald's executive

relegates it to the status of ornament—a nice accessory if you want it, so long as it doesn't get in the way of the important stuff. Yet by taking this view, Motivation 2.0 neglects a crucial part of who we are. From the moment that human beings first stared into the sky, contemplated their place in the universe, and tried to create something that bettered the world and outlasted their lives, we have been purpose seekers. "Purpose provides activation energy for living," psychologist Mihaly Csikszentmihalyi told me in an interview. "I think that evolution has had a hand in selecting people who had a sense of doing something beyond themselves."

Motivation 3.0 seeks to reclaim this aspect of the human condition. Baby boomers around the world—because of the stage of their lives and the size of their numbers—are nudging purpose closer to the cultural center. In response, business has begun to rethink how purpose figures in what it does. "As an emotional catalyst, wealth maximization lacks the power to fully mobilize human energies," says strategy guru (and boomer) Gary Hamel.[3] Those staggering levels of worker disengagement I described in the previous chapter have a companion trend that companies are only starting to recognize: an equally sharp rise in volunteerism, especially in the United States. These diverging lines—compensated engagement going down, uncompensated effort going up—suggest that volunteer work is nourishing people in ways that paid work simply is not.

We're learning that the profit motive, potent though it is, can be an insufficient impetus for both individuals and organizations. An equally powerful source of energy, one we've often neglected or dismissed as unrealistic, is what we might call the "purpose

motive." This is the final big distinction between the two operating systems. Motivation 2.0 centered on profit maximization. Motivation 3.0 doesn't reject profits, but it places equal emphasis on purpose maximization. We see the first stirrings of this new purpose motive in three realms of organizational life—goals, words, and policies.

Goals

Boomers aren't singing alone in their chorus of purpose. Joining them, and using the same hymnbook, are their sons and daughters— known as Generation Y, the millennials, or the echo boomers. These young adults, who have recently begun entering the workforce themselves, are shifting the center of gravity in organizations by their very presence. As the writer Sylvia Hewlett has found in her research, the two bookend generations "are redefining success [and] are willing to accept a radically 'remixed' set of rewards." Neither generation rates money as the most important form of compensation. Instead they choose a range of nonmonetary factors—from "a great team" to "the ability to give back to society through work."[4] And if they can't find that satisfying package of rewards in an existing organization, they'll create a venture of their own.

Take the case of American Gen Y-er Blake Mycoskie and TOMS

Shoes, the company he launched in 2006. TOMS doesn't fit snugly into the traditional business boxes. It offers hip, canvas, flat-soled shoes. But every time TOMS sells a pair of shoes to you, me, or your next-door neighbor, it gives away another pair of new shoes to a child in a developing country. Is TOMS a charity that finances its operation with shoe sales? Or is it a business that sacrifices its earnings in order to do good? It's neither—and it's both. The answer is so confusing, in fact, that TOMS Shoes had to address the question directly on its website, just below information on how to return a pair that's too big. TOMS, the site explains, is "a for-profit company with giving at its core."

Got it? No? Okay, try this: The company's "business model transforms our customers into benefactors." Better? Maybe. Weirder? Certainly. Ventures like TOMS blur, perhaps even shatter, the existing categories. Their goals, and the way companies reach them, are so incompatible to Motivation 2.0 that if TOMS had to rely on this twentieth-century operating system, the whole endeavor would seize up and crash in the entrepreneurial equivalent of a blue screen of death.

Motivation 3.0, by contrast, is expressly built for purpose maximization. In fact, the rise of purpose maximizers is one reason we need the new operating system in the first place. As I explained in Chapter 1, operations like TOMS are on the vanguard of a broader rethinking of how people organize what they do. "For benefit" organizations, B corporations, and low-profit limited-liability corporations all recast the goals of the traditional business enterprise. And all are becoming more prevalent as a new breed of businessperson seeks purpose with the fervor that traditional economic theory says entrepreneurs seek profit. Even cooperatives—an older business model with motives other than profit maximization—are moving from the shaggy edge to the clean-cut center. According to writer Marjorie Kelly, in the last three decades, worldwide membership in co-ops has doubled to 800 million people. In the United States alone, more people belong to a co-op than own shares in the stock market. And the idea is spreading. In Colombia, Kelly notes, "SaludCoop provides health-care services to a quarter of the population. In Spain, the Mondragón Corporación Cooperativa is the nation's seventh largest industrial concern."[5]

These "not only for profit" enterprises are a far cry from the "socially responsible" businesses that have been all the rage for the last fifteen years but have rarely delivered on their promise. The aims of these Motivation 3.0 companies are not to chase profit while trying to stay ethical and law-abiding. Their goal is to pursue purpose— and to use profit as the catalyst rather than the objective.

Words

In the spring of 2009, as the world economy was reeling from a once-in-a-generation crisis and the financial shenanigans that stoked it, a few Harvard Business School students glanced in the mirror and wondered if they were the problem. The people they'd aspired to be—financiers and corporate dealmakers—weren't, it turned out, heroes in an epic tale, but villains in a darker story. Many of these high-profile businesspeople were the ones who pushed the financial system to the brink. Meanwhile, these young men and women looked among their classmates and saw the seeds of similar behavior. In one survey of MBA students a few years earlier, a whopping 56 percent admitted to cheating regularly.[6]

So a handful of Harvard second-years, fearing that what was once a badge of honor had become three scarlet letters, did what business students are trained to do. They made a plan. Together they fashioned what they called "The MBA Oath"—a Hippocratic oath for business grads in which they pledge their fealty to causes above and beyond the bottom line. It's not a legal document. It's a code of conduct. And the conduct it recommends, as well as the very words it uses, leans more toward purpose maximization than profit maximization.

From the first sentence, the oath rings with the sounds of Motivation 3.0:

"As a manager, my purpose is to serve the greater good by bringing people and resources together to create value that no single individual can create alone," it begins. And on it goes for nearly five hundred words. "I will safeguard the interests of my shareholders, co-workers, customers and the society in which we operate," the oath-takers pledge. "I will strive to create sustainable economic, social, and environmental prosperity worldwide."

These words—"purpose," "greater good," "sustainable"—don't come from the Type X dictionary. One rarely hears them in business school—because, after all, that's not what business school is supposed to be about. Yet students at arguably the world's most powerful MBA factory thought otherwise. And in just a few weeks, roughly one-quarter of the graduating class had taken the oath and signed the pledge. In launching the effort, Max Anderson, one of the student founders, said: "My hope is that at our 25th reunion our class will not be known for how much money we made or how much money we gave back to the school, but for how the world was a better place as a result of our leadership."[7]

Words matter. And if you listen carefully, you might begin to hear a slightly different—slightly more purpose-oriented—dialect. Gary Hamel, whom I mentioned above, says, "The goals of management are usually described in words like 'efficiency,' 'advantage,' 'value,' 'superiority,' 'focus,' and 'differentiation.' Important as these objectives are, they lack the power to rouse human hearts." Business leaders, he says, "must find ways to infuse mundane business activities with deeper, soul-stirring ideals, such as honor, truth, love, justice, and beauty."[8] Humanize what people say and you may well humanize what they do.

That's the thinking behind the simple and effective way Robert B. Reich, former U.S. labor secretary, gauges the health of an organization. He calls it the "pronoun test." When he visits a workplace, he'll ask the people employed there some questions about the company. He listens to the substance of their response, of course. But most of all, he listens for the pronouns they use. Do the workers refer to the company as "they"? Or do they describe it in terms of "we"? "They" companies and "we" companies, he says, are very different places.[9] And in Motivation 3.0, "we" wins.

Policies

Between the words businesses use and the goals they seek sit the policies they implement to turn the former into the latter. Here, too, one can detect the early tremors of a different approach. For example, many companies in the last decade spent considerable time and effort crafting corporate ethics guidelines. Yet instances of unethical behavior don't seem to have declined. Valuable though those guidelines can be, as a policy they can unintentionally move purposeful behavior out of the Type I schema and into Type X. As Harvard Business School professor Max Bazerman has explained:

> Say you take people who are motivated to behave nicely, then give them a fairly weak set of ethical standards to meet. Now, instead of asking them to "do it because it's the right thing

139

> *"The value of a life can be measured by one's ability to affect the destiny of one less advantaged. Since death is an absolute certainty for everyone, the important variable is the quality of life one leads between the times of birth and death."*
>
> BILL STRICKLAND
> Founder of the Manchester
> Craftsmen's Guild, and MacArthur
> "genius award" winner

to do," you've essentially given them an alternate set of standards—do this so you can check off all these boxes.

Imagine an organization, for example, that believes in affirmative action—one that wants to make the world a better place by creating a more diverse workforce. By reducing ethics to a checklist, suddenly affirmative action is just a bunch of requirements that the organization must meet to show that it isn't discriminating.

Now the organization isn't focused on affirmatively pursuing diversity but rather on making sure that all the boxes are checked off to show that what it did is OK (and so it won't get sued). Before, its workers had an intrinsic motivation to do the right thing, but now they have an extrinsic motivation to make sure that the company doesn't get sued or fined.[10]

In other words, people might meet the minimal ethical standards to avoid punishment, but the guidelines have done nothing to inject purpose into the corporate bloodstream. The better approach could be to enlist the power of autonomy in the service of purpose maximization. Two intriguing examples demonstrate what I mean.

First, many psychologists and economists have found that the correlation between money and happiness is weak—that past a certain (and quite modest) level, a larger pile of cash doesn't bring people a higher level of satisfaction. But a few social scientists have begun adding a bit more nuance to this observation. According to Lara Aknin and Elizabeth Dunn, sociologists at the University of British Columbia, and Michael Norton, a psychologist at the Harvard Business School, *how* people spend their money may be at least as important as *how much* money they earn. In particular, spending money on other people (buying flowers for your spouse rather than an MP3 player for yourself) or on a cause (donating to a religious institution rather than going for an expensive haircut) can actually increase our subjective well-being.[11] In fact, Dunn and Norton propose turning their findings on what they call "pro-social" spending into corporate policy. According to *The Boston Globe*, they believe that "companies can improve their employees' emotional well-being by shifting some of their budget for charitable giving so that individual employees are given sums to donate, leaving them happier even as the charities of their choice benefit."[12] In other words, handing individual employees control over how the organization gives back to the community might do more to improve their overall satisfaction than one more "if-then" financial incentive.

Another study offers a second possible purpose-centered policy prescription. Physicians in high-profile settings like the Mayo Clinic face pressures and demands that can often lead to burnout. But field research at the prestigious medical facility found that letting doctors spend one day a week on the aspect of their job that was most meaningful to them—whether patient care, research, or community service—could reduce the physical and emotional exhaustion that accompanies their work. Doctors who participated in this trial policy had half the burnout rate of those who did not.[13] Think of it as "20 percent time" with a purpose.

THE GOOD LIFE

Each year about thirteen hundred seniors graduate from the University of Rochester and begin their journey into what many of their parents and professors like to call the real world. Edward Deci, Richard Ryan, and their colleague Christopher Niemiec decided to ask a sample of these soon-to-be graduates about their life goals—and then to follow up with them early in their careers to see how they were doing. While much social science research is done with student volunteers, scientists rarely track students after they've packed up their diplomas and exited the campus gates. And these researchers wanted to study the post-college time frame because it represents a "critical development period that marks people's transitions to their adult identities and lives."[14]

Some of the U of R students had what Deci, Ryan, and Niemiec label "extrinsic aspirations"—for instance, to become wealthy or to achieve fame—what we might call "profit goals." Others had "intrinsic aspirations"—to help others improve their lives, to learn, and to grow—or what we might think of as "purpose goals." After these students had been out in the real word for between one and two years, the researchers tracked them down to see how they were faring.

The people who'd had purpose goals and felt they were attaining them reported higher levels of satisfaction and subjective well-being than when they were in college, and quite low levels of anxiety and depression. That's probably no surprise. They'd set a personally meaningful goal and felt they were reaching it. In that situation, most of us would likely feel pretty good, too.

But the results for people with profit goals were more complicated. Those who said they were attaining their goals—accumulating wealth, winning acclaim—reported levels of satisfaction, self-esteem, and positive affect no higher than when they were students. In other words, they'd reached their goals, but it didn't make them any happier. What's more, gradu-

"One cannot lead a life that is truly excellent without feeling that one belongs to something greater and more permanent than oneself."

MIHALY CSIKSZENTMIHALYI

ates with profit goals showed *increases* in anxiety, depression, and other negative indicators—again, even though they were attaining their goals.

"These findings are rather striking," the researchers write, "as they suggest that attainment of a particular set of goals [in this case, profit goals] has no impact on well-being and actually contributes to ill-being."[15]

When I discussed these results with Deci and Ryan, they were especially emphatic about their significance—because the findings suggest that even when we *do* get what we want, it's not always what we need. "People who are very high in extrinsic goals for wealth are more likely to attain that wealth, but they're still unhappy," Ryan told me.

Or as Deci put it, "The typical notion is this: You value something. You attain it. Then you're better off as a function of it. But what we find is that there are certain things that if you value and if you attain them, you're *worse* off as a result of it, not better off."

Failing to understand this conundrum—that satisfaction depends not merely on having goals, but on having the right goals—can lead sensible people down self-destructive paths. If people chase profit goals, reach those goals, and still don't feel any better about their lives, one response is to increase the size and scope of the goals—to seek more money or greater outside validation. And that can "drive them down a road of further unhappiness thinking it's the road to happiness," Ryan said.

"One of the reasons for anxiety and depression in the high attainers is that they're not having good relationships. They're busy making money and attending to themselves and that means that there's less room in their lives for love and attention and caring and empathy and the things that truly count," Ryan added.

And if the broad contours of these findings are true for individuals, why shouldn't they also be true for organizations—which, of course, are collections of individuals? I don't mean to say that profit doesn't matter. It does. The profit motive has been an important fuel for achievement. But it's not the only motive. And it's not the most important one. Indeed, if we were to look at history's greatest achievements—from the printing press to constitutional democracy to cures for deadly diseases—the spark that kept the creators working deep into the night was purpose at least as much as profit. A healthy society—and healthy business organizations—begins with purpose and considers profit a way to move toward that end or a happy by-product of its attainment.

And here the boomers—maybe, just maybe—can take the lead. On the subjects of autonomy and mastery, adults should look to the eloquent example of children. But perhaps purpose is another matter. Being able to contemplate the big picture, to ponder one's own mortality, to understand the paradox that attaining certain goals isn't the answer seem to require having spent a few years on the planet. And since the planet very soon will contain more people over age sixty-five than under age five for the first time in its existence, the timing couldn't be better.

It's in our nature to seek purpose. But that nature is now being revealed and expressed on a scale that is demographically unprecedented and, until recently, scarcely imaginable. The consequences could rejuvenate our businesses and remake our world.

A CENTRAL IDEA of this book has been the mismatch between what science knows and what business does. The gap is wide. Its existence is alarming. And though closing it seems daunting, we have reasons to be optimistic.

The scientists who study human motivation, several of whom we've encountered in this book, offer us a sharper and more accurate account of both human performance and the human condition. The truths they've revealed are simple, yet powerful. The science shows that those typical twentieth-century carrot-and-stick motivators—things we consider somehow a "natural" part of human enterprise—can sometimes work. But they're effective in only a surprisingly narrow band of circumstances. The science shows that "if-then" rewards—the mainstays of the Motivation 2.0 operating system—not only are ineffective in many situations, but also can crush the high-level, creative, conceptual abilities that are central to current and future economic and social progress. The science shows that the secret to high performance isn't our biological drive or our reward-and-punishment drive, but our third drive—our deep-seated desire to direct our own lives, to extend and expand our abilities, and to live a life of purpose.

Bringing our businesses in sync with these truths won't be easy. Unlearning old ideas is difficult, undoing old habits even harder. And I'd be less sanguine about the prospects of closing the motivation gap anytime soon, if it weren't for this: The science confirms what we already know in our hearts.

We know that human beings are not merely smaller, slower, better-smelling horses galloping after that day's carrot. We know—if we've spent time with young children or remember ourselves at our best— that we're not destined to be passive and compliant. We're designed to be active and engaged. And we know that the richest experiences in our lives aren't when we're clamoring for validation from others, but when we're listening to our own voice—doing something that matters, doing it well, and doing it in the service of a cause larger than ourselves.

So, in the end, repairing the mismatch and bringing our understanding of motivation into the twenty-first century is more than an essential move for business. It's an affirmation of our humanity.

Part Three

The Type I Toolkit

Welcome to the Type I Toolkit.

This is your guide to taking the ideas in this book and putting them into action.

Whether you're looking for a better way to run your organization, navigate your career, or help your kids, there's a tip, a best practice, or a recommended book for you. And if ever you need a quick summary of Drive, or you want to look up one of its terms, you can find that here, too.

You don't have to read this section in any particular order. Pick an entry that interests you and dive right in. Like any good toolkit, this one is versatile enough for you to return to again and again.

P.S. I'd love to hear your suggestions for what to include in future editions of the Type I Toolkit. Send your ideas directly to me at dhp@danpink.com.

WHAT'S IN THIS TOOLKIT

Type I for Individuals. Nine Strategies for Awakening
Your Motivation

Type I for Organizations: Nine Ways to Improve Your
Company, Office, or Group

The Zen of Compensation: Paying People the
Type I Way

Type I for Parents and Educators: Nine Ideas
for Helping Our Kids

The Type I Reading List: Fifteen Essential Books

Listen to the Gurus: Six Business Thinkers Who Get It

The Type I Fitness Plan: Four Tips for Getting (and
Staying) Motivated to Exercise

Drive: The Recap

Drive: The Glossary

The *Drive* Discussion Guide: Twenty Conversation
Starters to Keep You Thinking and Talking

Find Out More—About Yourself and This Topic

Type I for Individuals:
Nine Strategies for Awakening
Your Motivation

Type I's are made, not born. Although the world is awash in extrinsic motivators, there's a lot we can do to bring more autonomy, mastery, and purpose into our work and life. Here are nine exercises to get you on the right track.

GIVE YOURSELF A "FLOW TEST"

Mihaly Csikszentmihalyi did more than discover the concept of "flow." He also introduced an ingenious new technique to measure it. Csikszentmihalyi and his University of Chicago team equipped participants in their research studies with electronic pagers. Then they paged people at random intervals (approximately eight times a day) for a week, asking them to describe their mental state at that moment. Compared with previous methods, these real-time reports proved far more honest and revealing.

You can use Csikszentmihalyi's methodological innovation in your own quest for mastery by giving yourself a "flow test." Set a reminder on your computer or mobile phone to go off at forty random times in a week. Each time your device beeps, write down what you're doing, how you're feeling, and whether you're in "flow." Record your observations, look at the patterns, and consider the following questions:

- Which moments produced feelings of "flow"? Where were you? What were you working on? Who were you with?
- Are certain times of day more flow-friendly than others? How could you restructure your day based on your findings?
- How might you increase the number of optimal experiences and reduce the moments when you felt disengaged or distracted?
- If you're having doubts about your job or career, what does this exercise tell you about your true source of intrinsic motivation?

FIRST, ASK A BIG QUESTION . . .

In 1962, Clare Boothe Luce, one of the first women to serve in the U.S. Congress, offered some advice to President John F. Kennedy. "A great man," she told him, "is one sentence." Abraham Lincoln's sentence was: "He preserved the union and freed the slaves." Franklin Roosevelt's was: "He lifted us out of a great depression and helped us win a world war." Luce feared that Kennedy's attention was so splintered among different priorities that his sentence risked becoming a muddled paragraph.

You don't have to be a president—of the United States or of your local gardening club—to learn from this tale. One way to orient your life toward greater purpose is to think about your sentence. Maybe it's: "He raised four kids who became happy and healthy adults." Or "She invented a device that made people's lives easier." Or "He cared for every person who walked into his office regardless of whether that person could pay." Or "She taught two generations of children how to read."

As you contemplate your purpose, begin with the big question: *What's your sentence?*

. . . THEN KEEP ASKING
A SMALL QUESTION

The big question is necessary, but not sufficient. That's where the small question comes in. Real achievement doesn't happen overnight. As anyone who's trained for a marathon, learned a new language, or run a successful division can attest, you spend a lot more time grinding through tough tasks than you do basking in applause.

Here's something you can do to keep yourself motivated. At the end of each day, ask yourself whether you were better today than you were yesterday. Did you do more? Did you do it well? Or to get specific, did you learn your ten vocabulary words, make your eight sales calls, eat your five servings of fruits and vegetables, write your four pages? You don't have to be flawless each day. Instead, look for small measures of improvement such as how long you practiced your saxophone or whether you held off on checking e-mail until you finished that report you needed to write. Reminding yourself that you don't need to be a master by day 3 is the best way of ensuring you will be one by day 3,000.

So before you go to sleep each night, ask yourself the small question: *Was I better today than yesterday?*

TAKE A SAGMEISTER

The designer Stefan Sagmeister has found a brilliant way to ensure he's living a Type I life. Think about the standard pattern in developed countries, he says. People usually spend the first twenty-five or so years of their lives learning, the next forty or so years working, and the final twenty-five in retirement. That boilerplate timeline got Sagmeister wondering: Why not snip five years from retirement and sprinkle them into your working years?

So every seven years, Sagmeister closes his graphic design shop, tells his clients he won't be back for a year, and goes off on a 365-day sabbatical. He uses the time to travel, to live places he's never been, and to experiment with new projects. It sounds risky, I know. But he says the ideas he generates during the year "off" often provide his income for the next seven years. "Taking a Sagmeister," as I now call it, requires a fair bit of planning and saving, of course. But doesn't forgoing that big-screen TV seem a small price to pay for an unforgettable—and un-get-backable—year of personal exploration? The truth is, this idea is more realistic than many of us realize. Which is why I hope to take a Sagmeister in a couple of years and why you should consider it, too.

GIVE YOURSELF A PERFORMANCE REVIEW

Performance reviews, those annual or biannual rituals of organizational life, are about as enjoyable as a toothache and as productive as a train wreck. Nobody likes them—not the giver, not the receiver. They don't really help us achieve mastery—since the feedback often comes six months after the work is complete. (Imagine Serena Williams or Twyla Tharp seeing their results or reading reviews only twice a year.) And yet managers keep on hauling employees into their offices for those awkward, painful encounters.

Maybe there's a better way. Maybe, as Douglas McGregor and others have suggested, we should give ourselves our own performance reviews. Here's how. Figure out your goals—mostly learning goals, but also a few performance goals—and then every month, call yourself to your office and give yourself an appraisal. How are you faring? Where are you falling short? What tools, information, or support might you need to do better?

Some other hints:

- Set both smaller and larger goals so that when it comes time to evaluate yourself you've already accomplished some whole tasks.
- Make sure you understand how every aspect of your work relates to your larger purpose.
- Be brutally honest. This exercise is aimed at helping you improve performance and achieve mastery—so if you rationalize failures or gloss over your mistakes instead of learning from them, you're wasting your time.

And if doing this solo isn't your thing, gather a small group of colleagues for regular peer-based do-it-yourself performance reviews. If your comrades really care, they'll tell you the truth and hold you accountable. One last question for bosses: Why in God's name are you not encouraging all your employees to do this?

GET UNSTUCK BY GOING OBLIQUE

Even the most intrinsically motivated person sometimes gets stuck. So here's a simple, easy, and fun way to power out of your mental morass. In 1975, producer Brian Eno and artist Peter Schmidt published a set of one hundred cards containing strategies that helped them overcome the pressure-packed moments that always accompany a deadline. Each card contains a single, often inscrutable, question or statement to push you out of a mental rut. (Some examples: *What would your closest friend do? Your mistake was a hidden intention. What is the simplest solution? Repetition is a form of change. Don't avoid what is easy.*) If you're working on a project and find yourself stymied, pull an Oblique card from the deck. These brain bombs are a great way to keep your mind open despite constraints you can't control. You can buy the deck at www.enoshop.co.uk/ or follow one of the Twitter accounts inspired by the strategies, such as: http://twitter.com/oblique_chirps.

MOVE FIVE STEPS CLOSER TO MASTERY

One key to mastery is what Florida State University psychology professor Anders Ericsson calls "deliberate practice"—a "lifelong period of . . . effort to improve performance in a specific domain."

Deliberate practice isn't running a few miles each day or banging on the piano for twenty minutes each morning. It's much more purposeful, focused, and, yes, painful. Follow these steps—over and over again for a decade—and you just might become a master:

- **Remember that deliberate practice has one objective: to improve performance.** "People who play tennis once a week for years don't get any better if they do the same thing each time," Ericsson has said. "Deliberate practice is about changing your performance, setting new goals and straining yourself to reach a bit higher each time."
- **Repeat, repeat, repeat.** Repetition matters. Basketball greats don't shoot ten free throws at the end of team practice; they shoot five hundred.
- **Seek constant, critical feedback.** If you don't know how you're doing, you won't know what to improve.
- **Focus ruthlessly on where you need help.** While many of us work on what we're already good at, says Ericsson, "those who get better work on their weaknesses."
- **Prepare for the process to be mentally and physically exhausting.** That's why so few people commit to it, but that's why it works.

TAKE A PAGE FROM WEBBER AND A CARD FROM YOUR POCKET

In his insightful book *Rules of Thumb*, *Fast Company* magazine cofounder Alan Webber offers a smart and simple exercise for assessing whether you're on the path to autonomy, mastery, and purpose. Get a few blank three-by-five-inch cards. On one of the cards, write your answer to this question: "What gets you up in the morning?" Now, on the other side of the card, write your answer to another question: "What keeps you up at night?" Pare each response to a single sentence. And if you don't like an answer, toss the card and try again until you've crafted something you can live with. Then read what you've produced. If both answers give you a sense of meaning and direction, "Congratulations!" says Webber. "Use them as your compass, checking from time to time to see if they're still true. If you don't like one or both of your answers, it opens up a new question: What are you going to do about it?"

CREATE YOUR OWN MOTIVATIONAL POSTER

Office posters that try to "motivate" us have a grim reputation. As one wag put it, "For the last two decades, motivational posters have inflicted unimaginable suffering on the workplaces of the world." But who knows? Perhaps the first one was a thing of beauty. Maybe those cave drawings in Lascaux, France, were some Paleolithic motivational speaker's way of saying, "If you know where you're going, you'll never take a wrong turn." Now you've got a chance to fight back (or perhaps to reclaim that ancient legacy). Thanks to a number of websites, you can create your own motivational posters—and you no longer have to settle for photos of kittens climbing out of baskets. You can be as serious or silly with this exercise as you like. Motivation is deeply personal and only you know what words or images will resonate with you.

Try any of these sites:

Despair Inc (http://diy.despair.com/motivator.php)
Big Huge Labs (http://bighugelabs.com/motivator.php)
Automotivator (http://wigflip.com/automotivator/)

To offer you some, er, motivation, here are two posters I created myself:

Type I for Organizations:
Nine Ways to Improve Your Company,
Office, or Group

Whether you're the CEO or the new intern, you can help create engaging, productive workplaces that foster Type I behavior. Here are nine ways to begin pulling your organization out of the past and into the brighter world of Motivation 3.0.

TRY "20 PERCENT TIME" WITH TRAINING WHEELS

You've read about the wonders of "20 percent time"—where organizations encourage employees to spend one-fifth of their hours working on any project they want. And if you've ever used Gmail or read Google News, you've benefited from the results. But for all the virtues of this Type I innovation, putting such a policy in place can seem daunting. How much will it cost? What if it doesn't work? If you're feeling skittish, here's an idea: Go with a more modest version—20 percent time . . . with training wheels. Start with, say,

10 percent time. That's just one afternoon of a five-day workweek. (Who among us hasn't wasted that amount of time at work anyway?) And instead of committing to it forever, try it for six months. By creating this island of autonomy, you'll help people act on their great ideas and convert their downtime into more productive time. And who knows? Someone in your operation just might invent the next Post-it note.

ENCOURAGE PEER-TO-PEER "NOW THAT" REWARDS

Kimley-Horn and Associates, a civil engineering firm in Raleigh, North Carolina, has established a reward system that gets the Type I stamp of approval: At any point, without asking permission, anyone in the company can award a $50 bonus to any of her colleagues. "It works because it's real-time, and it's not handed down from any management," the firm's human resources director told *Fast Company*. "Any employee who does something exceptional receives recognition from their peers within minutes." Because these bonuses are noncontingent "now that" rewards, they avoid the seven deadly flaws of most corporate carrots. And because they come from a colleague, not a boss, they carry a different (and perhaps deeper) meaning. You could even say they're motivating.

CONDUCT AN AUTONOMY AUDIT

How much autonomy do the people in your organization really have? If you're like most folks, you probably don't have a clue. Nobody does. But there's a way to find out—with an autonomy audit.

Ask everyone in your department or on your team to respond to these four questions with a numerical ranking (using a scale of 0 to 10, with 0 meaning "almost none" and 10 meaning "a huge amount"):

1. *How much autonomy do you have over your tasks at work— your main responsibilities and what you do in a given day?*

2. *How much autonomy do you have over your time at work— for instance, when you arrive, when you leave, and how you allocate your hours each day?*

3. *How much autonomy do you have over your team at work— that is, to what extent are you able to choose the people with whom you typically collaborate?*

4. *How much autonomy do you have over your technique at work—how you actually perform the main responsibilities of your job?*

Make sure all responses are anonymous. Then tabulate the results. What's the employee average? The figure will fall somewhere on a 40-point autonomy scale (with 0 being a North Korean prison and 40 being Woodstock). Compare that number to people's perceptions. Perhaps the boss thought everyone had plenty of freedom—but the audit showed an average autonomy rating of only 15. Also calculate separate results for task, time, team, and technique. A healthy overall average can sometimes mask a problem in a particular area. An overall autonomy rating of, say, 27 isn't bad. However, if that average consists of 8 each for task, technique, and team, but only 3 for time, you've identified an autonomy weak spot in the organization.

It's remarkable sometimes how little the people running organizations know about the experiences of the people working around them. But it's equally remarkable how often leaders are willing to do things differently if they see real data. That's what an autonomy audit can do. And if you include a section in your audit for employees to jot down their own ideas about increasing autonomy, you might even find some great solutions.

TAKE THREE STEPS TOWARD GIVING UP CONTROL

Type X bosses relish control. Type I bosses *relinquish* control. Extending people the freedom they need to do great work is usually wise, but it's not always easy. So if you're feeling the urge to control, here are three ways to begin letting go—for your own benefit and your team's:

1. **Involve people in goal-setting.** Would you rather set your own goals or have them foisted upon you? Thought so. Why should those working with you be any different? A considerable body of research shows that individuals are far more engaged when they're pursuing goals they had a hand in creating. So bring employees into the process. They could surprise you: People often have higher aims than the ones you assign them.

2. **Use noncontrolling language.** Next time you're about to say "must" or "should," try saying "think about" or "consider" instead. A small change in wording can help promote engagement over compliance and might even reduce some people's urge to defy. Think about it. Or at least consider it, okay?

3. **Hold office hours.** Sometimes you need to summon people into your office. But sometimes it's wise to let

them come to you. Take a cue from college professors and set aside one or two hours a week when your schedule is clear and any employee can come in and talk to you about anything that's on her mind. Your colleagues might benefit and you might learn something.

PLAY "WHOSE PURPOSE IS IT ANYWAY?"

This is another exercise designed to close the gap between perception and reality. Gather your team, your department, or, if you can, all the employees in your outfit. Hand everyone a blank three-by-five-inch card. Then ask each person to write down his or her one-sentence answer to the following question: "What is our company's (or organization's) purpose?" Collect the cards and read them aloud. What do they tell you? Are the answers similar, everyone aligned along a common purpose? Or are they all over the place—some people believing one thing, others something completely different, and still others without even a guess? For all the talk about culture, alignment, and mission, most organizations do a pretty shabby job of assessing this aspect of their business. This simple inquiry can offer a glimpse into the soul of your enterprise. If people don't know why they're doing what they're doing, how can you expect them to be motivated to do it?

USE REICH'S PRONOUN TEST

Former U.S. labor secretary Robert B. Reich has devised a smart, simple, (and free) diagnostic tool for measuring the health of an organization. When he talks to employees, he listens carefully for the pronouns they use. Do employees refer to their company as "they" or as "we"? "They" suggests at least some amount of disengagement, and perhaps even alienation. "We" suggests the opposite—that employees feel they're part of something significant and meaningful. If you're a boss, spend a few days listening to the people around you, not only in formal settings like meetings, but in the hallways and at lunch as well. Are you a "we" organization or a "they" organization? The difference matters. Everybody wants autonomy, mastery, and purpose. The thing is, "we" can get it—but "they" can't.

DESIGN FOR INTRINSIC MOTIVATION

Internet guru and author Clay Shirky (www.shirky.com) says that the most successful websites and electronic forums have a certain Type I approach in their DNA. They're designed—often explicitly—to tap intrinsic motivation. You can do the same with your online presence if you listen to Shirky and:

- Create an environment that makes people feel good about participating.
- Give users autonomy.
- Keep the system as open as possible.

And what matters in cyberspace matters equally in physical space. Ask yourself: How does the built environment of your workplace promote or inhibit autonomy, mastery, and purpose?

PROMOTE GOLDILOCKS FOR GROUPS

Almost everyone has experienced the satisfaction of a Goldilocks task—the kind that's neither too easy nor too hard, that delivers a delicious sense of flow. But sometimes it's difficult to replicate that experience when you're working in a team. People often end up doing the jobs they always do because they've proven they can do them well, and an unfortunate few get saddled with the flow-free tasks nobody else wants. Here are a few ways to bring a little Goldilocks to your group:

- **Begin with a diverse team.** As Harvard's Teresa Amabile advises, "Set up work groups so that people will stimulate each other and learn from each other, so that they're not homogeneous in terms of their backgrounds and training. You want people who can really cross-fertilize each other's ideas."
- **Make your group a "no competition" zone.** Pitting coworkers against one another in the hope that competition will spark them to perform better rarely works— and almost always undermines intrinsic motivation. If you're going to use a c-word, go with "collaboration" or "cooperation."
- **Try a little task-shifting.** If someone is bored with his current assignment, see if he can train someone else in the skills he's already mastered. Then see if he can take on some aspect of a more experienced team member's work.
- **Animate with purpose, don't motivate with rewards.** Nothing bonds a team like a shared mission. The more

that people share a common cause—whether it's creating something insanely great, outperforming an outside competitor, or even changing the world—the more your group will do deeply satisfying and outstanding work.

TURN YOUR NEXT OFF-SITE INTO A FEDEX DAY

Behold the company off-site, a few spirit-sapping days of forced fun and manufactured morale—featuring awkward pep talks, wretched dancing, and a few "trust falls." To be fair, some off-sites reengage employees, recharge people's batteries, and restart conversations on big issues. But if your organization's off-sites are falling short, why not try replacing the next one with a FedEx Day? Set aside an entire day where employees can work on anything they choose, however they want, with whomever they'd like. Make sure they have the tools and resources they need. And impose just one rule: People must deliver something—a new idea, a prototype of a product, a better internal process—the following day. Type I organizations know what their Type X counterparts rarely comprehend: Real challenges are far more invigorating than controlled leisure.

The Zen of Compensation:
Paying People the Type I Way

Everybody wants to be paid well. I sure do. I bet you're the same. The Type I approach to motivation doesn't require bargain basement wages or an all-volunteer workforce, but it does demand a new approach to pay.

Think of this new approach as the Zen of compensation: In Motivation 3.0, the best use of money is to take the issue of money off the table.

The more prominent salary, perks, and benefits are in someone's work life, the more they can inhibit creativity and unravel performance. As Edward Deci explained in Chapter 3, when organizations use rewards like money to motivate staff, "that's when they're most demotivating." The better strategy is to get compensation right—and then get it out of sight. Effective organizations compensate people in amounts and in ways that allow individuals to mostly forget about compensation and instead focus on the work itself.

Here are three key techniques.

1. ENSURE INTERNAL AND EXTERNAL FAIRNESS

The most important aspect of any compensation package is fairness. And here, fairness comes in two varieties—internal and external. Internal fairness means paying people commensurate with their colleagues. External fairness means paying people in line with others doing similar work in similar organizations.

Let's look at each type of fairness. Suppose you and Fred have adjoining cubicles. And suppose you've got pretty much equivalent responsibility and experience. If Fred makes scads more money than you, you'll be miffed. Because of this violation of internal fairness, your motivation will plummet. Now suppose instead that you and Fred are both auditors with ten years' experience working in a Fortune 200 company. If you discover that similarly experienced auditors at other Fortune 200 firms are making double your salaries, both you and Fred will experience a largely irreversible motivation dip. The company has violated the ethic of external fairness. (One important addendum: Paying people the Type I way doesn't mean paying everyone the same amount. If Fred has a harder job or contributes more to the organization than you, he deserves a richer deal. And, as it turns out, several studies have shown that most people don't have a beef with that. Why? It's fair.)

Getting the internal and external equity right isn't itself a motivator. But it is a way to avoid putting the issue of money back on the table and making it a *de*-motivator.

2. PAY MORE THAN AVERAGE

If you have provided adequate baseline rewards and established internal and external fairness, consider borrowing a strategy first surfaced by a Nobel laureate. In the mid-1980s, George Akerlof, who later won the Nobel Prize in economics, and his wife, Janet Yellen, who's also an economist, discovered that some companies seemed to be overpaying their workers. Instead of paying employees the wages that supply and demand would have predicted, they gave their workers a little more. It wasn't because the companies were selfless and it wasn't because they were stupid. It was because they were savvy. Paying great people a little more than the market demands, Akerlof and Yellen found, could attract better talent, reduce turnover, and boost productivity and morale.

Higher wages could actually *reduce* a company's costs.

The pay-more-than-average approach can offer an elegant way to bypass "if-then" rewards, eliminate concerns about unfairness, and help take the issue of money off the table. It's another way to allow people to focus on the work itself. Indeed, other economists have shown that providing an employee a high level of base pay does more to boost performance and organizational commitment than an attractive bonus structure.

Of course, by the very nature of the exercise, paying above the average will work for only about half of you. So get going before your competitors do.

3. IF YOU USE PERFORMANCE METRICS, MAKE THEM WIDE-RANGING, RELEVANT, AND HARD TO GAME

Imagine you're a product manager and your pay depends largely on reaching a particular sales goal for the next quarter. If you're smart, or if you've got a family to feed, you're going to try mightily to hit that number. You probably won't concern yourself much with the quarter after that or the health of the company or whether the firm is investing enough in research and development. And if you're nervous, you might cut corners to reach your quarterly goal.

Now imagine you're a product manager and your pay is determined by these factors: your sales for the next quarter; your sales in the current year; the company's revenue and profit in the next two years; levels of satisfaction among your customers; ideas for new products; and evaluations of your coworkers. If you're smart, you'll probably try to sell your product, serve your customers, help your teammates, and, well, do good work. When metrics are varied, they're harder to finagle.

In addition, the gain for reaching the metrics shouldn't be too large. When the payoff for reaching targets is modest, rather than massive, it's less likely to narrow people's focus or encourage them to take the low road.

To be sure, finding the right mix of metrics is difficult and will vary considerably across organizations. And some people will inevitably find a way to game even the most carefully calibrated system. But using a variety of measures that reflect the totality of great work can transform often counterproductive "if-then" rewards into less combustible "now that" rewards.

Type I for Parents and Educators:
Nine Ideas for Helping Our Kids

All kids start out as curious, self-directed Type I's. But many of them end up as disengaged, compliant Type X's. What's going on? Maybe the problem is us—the adults who are running schools and heading families. If we want to equip young people for the new world of work—and, more important, if we want them to lead satisfying lives—we need to break Motivation 2.0's grip on education and parenting.

Unfortunately, as with business, there's a mismatch between what science knows and what schools do. Science knows (and you do, too, if you read Chapter 2) that if you promise a preschooler a fancy certificate for drawing a picture, that child will likely draw a picture for you—and then lose further interest in drawing. Yet in the face of this evidence—and as the world economy demands more nonroutine, creative, conceptual abilities—too many schools are moving in the wrong direction. They're redoubling their emphasis on routines, right answers, and standardization. And they're hauling out a wagon full of "if-then" rewards—pizza for reading books, iPods for showing up to class, cash for good test scores. We're bribing students into compliance instead of challenging them into engagement.

We can do better. And we should. If we want to raise Type I kids, at school and at home, we need to help them move toward autonomy, mastery, and purpose. Here are nine ways to start the journey.

APPLY THE THREE-PART TYPE I TEST FOR HOMEWORK

Does the homework bulging from kids' backpacks truly help them learn? Or does it simply steal their free time in the service of a false sense of rigor? Teachers, before you dole out yet another time-consuming assignment, run it through this Type I homework test by asking yourself three questions:

- Am I offering students any autonomy over how and when to do this work?
- Does this assignment promote mastery by offering a novel, engaging task (as opposed to rote reformulation of something already covered in class)?
- Do my students understand the purpose of this assignment? That is, can they see how doing this additional activity at home contributes to the larger enterprise in which the class is engaged?

If the answer to any of these questions is no, can you refashion the assignment? And parents, are you looking at homework assignments every so often to see whether they promote compliance or engagement? Let's not waste our kids' time on meaningless exercises. With a little thought and effort, we can turn home*work* into home*learning*.

HAVE A FedEx DAY

In Chapter 4, we learned how the software company Atlassian injects a burst of autonomy into its workplace by setting aside a day each quarter when employees can work on any project they choose, however they want, with whomever they'd like. Why not try this with your students—or even your own sons and daughters? Set aside an entire school day (or a family vacation day) and ask kids to come up with a problem to solve or a project to tackle. In advance, help them collect the tools, information, and supplies they might need. Then let them have at it. The next morning, ask them to deliver—by reporting back to the class or the family on their discoveries and experiences. It's like *Project Runway*—only the kids come up with the project themselves, and the reward at the end of the day is the chance to share what they've created and all they've learned along the way.

TRY DIY REPORT CARDS

Too many students walk through the schoolhouse door with one aim in mind: to get good grades. And all too often, the best way to reach this goal is to get with the program, avoid risks, and serve up the answers the teacher wants the way the teacher wants them. Good grades become a reward for compliance—but don't have much to do with learning. Meanwhile, students whose grades don't measure up often see themselves as failures and give up trying to learn.

The Type I approach is different. Report cards are not a potential prize, but a way to offer students useful feedback on their progress. And Type I students understand that a great way to get feedback is to evaluate their own progress.

So try experimenting with the DIY (do it yourself) report card. At the beginning of a semester, ask students to list their top learning goals. Then, at the end of the semester, ask them to create their own report card along with a one- or two-paragraph review of their progress. Where did they succeed? Where did they fall short? What more do they need to learn? Once students have completed their DIY report cards, show them the teacher's report card, and let the comparison of the two be the start of a conversation on how they are doing on their path toward mastery. Maybe even include students in any parent-teacher conferences. (Parents: If your child's teacher won't go for these DIY report cards, try it yourself at home. It's another way to prevent school from changing your child's default setting and turning him from Type I to Type X.)

GIVE YOUR KIDS AN ALLOWANCE AND SOME CHORES—BUT DON'T COMBINE THEM

Here's why an allowance is good for kids: Having a little of their own money, and deciding how to save or spend it, offers a measure of autonomy and teaches them to be responsible with cash.

Here's why household chores are good for kids: Chores show kids that families are built on mutual obligations and that family members need to help each other.

Here's why combining allowances with chores is *not* good for kids. By linking money to the completion of chores, parents turn an allowance into an "if-then" reward. This sends kids a clear (and clearly wrongheaded) message: In the absence of a payment, no self-respecting child would willingly set the table, empty the garbage, or make her own bed. It converts a moral and familial obligation into just another commercial transaction—and teaches that the only reason to do a less-than-desirable task for your family is in exchange for payment. This is a case where combining two good things give you less, not more. So keep allowance and chores separate, and you just might get that trash can emptied. Even better, your kids will begin to learn the difference between principles and payoffs.

OFFER PRAISE . . . THE RIGHT WAY

Done right, praise is an important way to give kids feedback and encouragement. But done wrong, praise can become yet another "if-then" reward that can squash creativity and stifle intrinsic motivation.

The powerful work of psychologist Carol Dweck, as well as others in the field, offers a how-to list for offering praise in a way that promotes Type I behavior:

- **Praise effort and strategy, not intelligence.** As Dweck's research has shown, children who are praised for "being smart" often believe that every encounter is a test of whether they really are. So to avoid looking dumb, they resist new challenges and choose the easiest path. By contrast, kids who understand that effort and hard work lead to mastery and growth are more willing to take on new, difficult tasks.

- **Make praise specific.** Parents and teachers should give kids useful information about their performance. Instead of bathing them in generalities, tell them specifically what they've done that's noteworthy.

- **Praise in private.** Praise is feedback—not an award ceremony. That's why it's often best to offer it one-on-one, in private.

- **Offer praise only when there's a good reason for it.** Don't kid a kid. He can see through fake praise in a nanosecond. Be sincere—or keep quiet. If you overpraise, kids regard it as dishonest and unearned. Plus, overpraising becomes another "if-then" reward that makes earning praise, rather than moving toward mastery, the objective.

HELP KIDS SEE THE BIG PICTURE

In education systems tilted toward standardized tests, grades, and "if-then" rewards, students often have no idea why they're doing what they're doing. Turn that around by helping them glimpse the big picture. Whatever they're studying, be sure they can answer these questions: *Why am I learning this? How is it relevant to the world I live in now?* Then get out of the classroom and apply what they're studying. If they're learning Spanish, take them to an office, a store, or a community center where they can actually speak the language. If they're studying geometry, have them draw up architectural plans for an addition to your school or home. If they're taking history, ask them to apply what they've learned to an event in the news. Think of it as the fourth R: reading, writing, arithmetic . . . and relevance.

CHECK OUT THESE FIVE TYPE I SCHOOLS

Although most schools around the world are still built atop the Motivation 2.0 operating system, a number of forward-thinking educators have long understood that young people are brimming with the third drive. Here are five Type I schools in the United States with practices to emulate and stories to inspire.

- **Big Picture Learning.** Since 1996, with the opening of its flagship public high school, the Met, in Providence, Rhode Island, Big Picture Learning has been creating places that cultivate engagement rather than demand compliance. Founded by two veteran education innovators, Dennis Littky and Elliot Washor, Big Picture is a nonprofit that now has sixty-plus schools around the United States that put students in charge of their own education. Big Picture kids get the basics. But they also *use* those basics and acquire other skills by doing real work in the community—all under the guidance of an experienced adult tutor. And instead of easily gamed Motivation 2.0 measurements, Big Picture kids are assessed the way adults are—on work performance, individual presentations, effort, attitude, and behavior on the job. Most of the students at the Met and other Big Picture schools are "at risk" low-income and minority kids who've been poorly served by conventional schools. Yet thanks to this innovative Type I approach, more than 95 percent graduate and go on to college. For more information, go to http://www.bigpicture.org/. (Full disclosure: I have served, unpaid, on the board of directors of Big Picture since 2007.)

- **Sudbury Valley School.** Take a look at this independent school in Framingham, Massachusetts, to see what happens when young kids have genuine autonomy. Working from the assumption that all human beings are naturally curious and that the best kind of learning happens when it's initiated and pursued by the one doing the learning, Sudbury Valley School gives its students total control over the task, time, and technique of their learning. Teachers and staff are there to help them make things happen. This is a school where engagement is the rule and compliance isn't an option. For more information, go to http://www.sudval.org/.

- **The Tinkering School.** More of a lab than a school, this summer program, created by computer scientist Gever Tulley, lets children from seven to seventeen play around with interesting stuff and build cool things. At the headquarters in Montara, California, Tulley's tinkerers have built: working zip-lines, motorcycles, toothbrush robots, roller coasters, and plastic bag bridges strong enough to hold people. Most of us aren't able to ship our kids out to California for a week of tinkering, but we can all learn the "Five Dangerous Things You Should Let Your Children Do." So take nine minutes to listen to Tulley's 2007 online TED Talk of that title. Then hand your kids a pocket-knife, some power tools, and a book of matches—and get out of the way. For more information, go to http://www .tinkeringschool.com/ (includes a link to Tulley's talk).

- **Puget Sound Community School.** Like Sudbury and Big Picture, this tiny independent school in Seattle, Washington, gives its students a radical dose of autonomy, turning the "one size fits all" approach of conventional schools on its head. Each student has an adviser who acts as her personal coach, helping her come up with her own learning goals. "School" consists of a mixture of class time and self-created independent study projects, along with community service devised by the students. Since youngsters are often away from campus, they gain a clear sense that their learning has a real-world purpose. And rather than chase after grades, they receive frequent, informal feedback from advisers, teachers, and peers. For more information, go to www.pscs.org.

- **Montessori Schools.** Dr. Maria Montessori developed the Montessori method of teaching in the early 1900s after observing children's natural curiosity and innate desire to learn. Her early understanding of the third drive spawned a worldwide network of schools, mostly for preschool and primary-aged children. Many of the key tenets of a Montessori education resonate with the principles of Motivation 3.0—that children naturally engage in self-directed learning and independent study; that teachers should act as observers and facilitators of that learning, and not as lecturers or commanders; and that children are naturally inclined to experience periods of intense focus, concentration, and flow that adults should do their best not to interrupt. Although Montessori schools are rare at the junior high and high school levels, every school, educator, and parent can learn from its enduring and successful approach. Meantime, while you're investigating

Montessori, check out two other approaches to learning that also promote Type I behavior: the Reggio Emilia philosophy for the education of young children and the Waldorf schools. For more information, visit these websites: www.montessori-ami.org, www.montessori.org, www.amshq.org, www.reggioalliance.org, and www .whywaldorfworks.org.

TAKE A CLASS FROM THE UNSCHOOLERS

In the United States, the homeschooling movement has been growing at a remarkable pace over the past twenty years. And the fastest-growing segment of that movement is the "unschoolers"— families that don't use a formal curriculum and instead allow their children to explore and learn what interests them. Unschoolers have been among the first to adopt a Type I approach to education. They promote autonomy by allowing youngsters to decide what they learn and how they learn it. They encourage mastery by allowing children to spend as long as they'd like and to go as deep as they desire on the topics that interest them. Even if unschooling is not for you or your kids, you can learn a thing or two from these educational innovators. Start by reading John Taylor Gatto's extraordinary book, *Dumbing Us Down*. Take a look at *Home Education Magazine* and its website. Then check out some of the many other unschooling sites on the Web. For more information, go to www.homeedmag.com, www .unschooling.com, and www.sandratodd.com/unschooling.

TURN STUDENTS INTO TEACHERS

One of the best ways to know whether you've mastered something is to try to teach it. Give students that opportunity. Assign each pupil in a class a different aspect of the broader topic you're studying—and then have them take turns teaching what they've learned to their classmates. And once they've got it down, give them a wider audience by inviting other classes, teachers, parents, or school administrators to learn what they have to teach.

Also, at the start of a school term, ask students about their individual passions and areas of expertise. Keep a list of your experts, and then call upon them as needed throughout the term. A classroom of teachers is a classroom of learners.

The Type I Reading List:
Fifteen Essential Books

Autonomy, mastery, and purpose are integral to the human condition, so it's no surprise that a number of writers—from psychologists to journalists to novelists—have explored these three elements and probed what they mean for our lives. This list of books, arranged alphabetically by author, isn't exhaustive—but it's a good starting point for anyone interested in cultivating a Type I life.

Finite and Infinite Games:
A Vision of Life as Play and Possibility
BY JAMES P. CARSE

In his elegant little book, religious scholar Carse describes two types of games. A "finite game" has a winner and an end; the goal is to triumph. An "infinite game" has no winner and no end; the goal is to keep playing. Nonwinnable games, Carse explains, are much more rewarding than the win-lose ones we're accustomed to playing at our work and in our relationships.

Type I Insight: "Finite players play within boundaries; infinite players play with boundaries."

Talent Is Overrated: What Really Separates World-Class Performers from Everybody Else
BY GEOFF COLVIN

What's the difference between those who are pretty good at what they do and those who are masters? *Fortune* magazine's Colvin scours the evidence and shows that the answer is threefold: practice, practice, practice. But it's not just any practice, he says. The secret is "deliberate practice"—highly repetitive, mentally demanding work that's often unpleasant, but undeniably effective.

Type I Insight: "If you set a goal of becoming an expert in your business, you would immediately start doing all kinds of things you don't do now."

Flow: The Psychology of Optimal Experience
BY MIHALY CSIKSZENTMIHALYI

It's tough to find a better argument for working hard at something you love than Csikszentmihalyi's landmark book on "optimal experiences." *Flow* describes those exhilarating moments when we feel in control, full of purpose, and in the zone. And it reveals how people have turned even the most unpleasant tasks into enjoyable, rewarding challenges.

Type I Insight: "Contrary to what we usually believe . . . the best moments in our lives are not the passive, receptive, relaxing times—although such experiences can also be enjoyable, if we have worked hard to attain them. The best moments usually occur when a person's body or mind is stretched to the limits in a voluntary effort to accomplish something difficult and worthwhile."

For more of Csikszentmihalyi's ideas, check out three of his other books: *Finding Flow: The Psychology of Engagement with Everyday Life; Creativity: Flow and the Psychology of Discovery and Invention;* and the classic *Beyond Boredom and Anxiety: Experiencing Flow in Work and Play.*

Why We Do What We Do: Understanding Self-Motivation
BY EDWARD L. DECI WITH RICHARD FLASTE

In 1995, Edward Deci wrote a short book that introduced his powerful theories to a popular audience. In clear, readable prose, he discusses the limitations of a society based on control, explains the origins of his landmark experiments, and shows how to promote autonomy in the many realms of our lives.

Type I Insight: "The questions so many people ask—namely, 'How do I motivate people to learn? to work? to do their chores? or to take their medicine?'—are the wrong questions. They are wrong because they imply that motivation is something that gets done to people rather than something that people do."

Mindset: The New Psychology of Success
BY CAROL DWECK

Stanford's Dweck distills her decades of research to a simple pair of ideas. People can have two different mindsets, she says. Those with a "fixed mindset" believe that their talents and abilities are carved in stone. Those with a "growth mindset" believe that their talents and abilities can be developed. Fixed mindsets see every encounter as a test of their worthiness. Growth mindsets see the same encounters as opportunities to improve. Dweck's message: Go with growth.

Type I Insight: In the book and likewise on her website, www .mindsetonline.com, Dweck offers concrete steps for moving from a fixed to a growth mindset:

- Learn to listen for a fixed mindset "voice" that might be hurting your resiliency.
- Interpret challenges not as roadblocks, but as opportunities to stretch yourself.
- Use the language of growth—for example, "I'm not sure I can do it now, but I think I can learn with time and effort."

Then We Came to the End
BY JOSHUA FERRIS

This darkly hilarious debut novel is a cautionary tale for the demoralizing effects of the Type X workplace. At an unnamed ad agency in Chicago, people spend more time scarfing free doughnuts and scamming office chairs than doing actual work—all while fretting about "walking Spanish down the hall," office lingo for being fired.

Type I Insight: "They had taken away our flowers, our summer days, and our bonuses, we were on a wage freeze and a hiring freeze and people were flying out the door like so many dismantled dummies. We had one thing still going for us: the prospect of a promotion. A new title: true, it came with no money, the power was almost always illusory, the bestowal a cheap shrewd device concocted by management to keep us from mutiny, but when word circulated that one of us had jumped up an acronym, that person was just a little quieter that day, took a longer lunch than usual, came back with shopping bags, spent the afternoon speaking softly into the telephone, and left whenever they wanted that night, while the rest of us sent emails flying back and forth on the lofty topics of Injustice and Uncertainty."

Good Work: When Excellence and Ethics Meet
BY HOWARD GARDNER, MIHALY CSIKSZENTMIHALYI, AND WILLIAM DAMON

How can you do "good work" in an age of relentless market forces and lightning-fast technology? By considering three basic issues: your profession's *mission*, its *standards* or "best practices," and your own *identity*. Although this book focuses mainly on examples from the fields of genetics and journalism, its insights can be applied to a number of professions buffeted by changing times. The authors have also continued their effort to identify individuals and institutions that exemplify "good work" on their website: www.goodwork.org.

Type I Insight: "What do you do if you wake up in the morning and dread going to work, because the daily routine no longer satisfies your standards?"

- Start groups or forums with others in your industry or outside it to reach beyond your current area of influence.
- Work with existing organizations to confirm your profession's values or develop new guidelines.
- Take a stand. It can be risky, sure, but leaving a job for ethical reasons need not involve abandoning your professional goals.

Outliers: The Story of Success
BY MALCOLM GLADWELL

With a series of compelling and gracefully told stories, Gladwell deftly takes a hammer to the idea of the "self-made man." Success is more complicated, he says. High achievers—from young Canadian hockey players to Bill Gates to the Beatles—are often the products of hidden advantages of culture, timing, demographics, and luck that helped them become masters in their fields. Reading this book will lead you to reevaluate your own path. More important, it will make you wonder how much human potential we're losing when so many people are denied these advantages.

Type I Insight: "It is not how much money we make that ultimately makes us happy between nine-to-five. It's whether our work fulfills us. If I offered you a choice between being an architect for $75,000 a year and working in a tollbooth every day for the rest of your life for $100,000 a year, which would you take? I'm guessing the former, because there is complexity, autonomy, and a relationship between effort and reward in doing creative work, and that's worth more to most of us than money."

Team of Rivals: The Political Genius of Abraham Lincoln
BY DORIS KEARNS GOODWIN

In her entertaining popular history, Goodwin shows Abraham Lincoln as an exemplar of Type I behavior. He worked mightily to achieve mastery in law and politics. He gave his staunchest rivals power and autonomy. And he developed a leadership style rooted in a higher purpose—ending slavery and keeping the union intact.

Type I Insight: Goodwin sheds light on Lincoln's Type I leadership skills. Among them:

- He was self-confident enough to surround himself with rivals who excelled in areas where he was weak.
- He genuinely listened to other people's points of view, which helped him form more complex opinions of his own.
- He gave credit where it was due and wasn't afraid to take the blame.

The Amateurs: The Story of Four Young Men and Their Quest for an Olympic Gold Medal
BY DAVID HALBERSTAM

What would compel a group of men to endure untold physical pain and exhaustion for a sport that promised no monetary compensation or fame? That's the question at the heart of Halberstam's riveting narrative about the 1984 U.S. rowing trials, a book that offers a glimpse into the fires of intrinsic motivation.

Type I Insight: "No chartered planes or buses ferried the athletes into Princeton. No team managers hustled their baggage from the bus to the hotel desk and made arrangements so that at mealtime they need only show up and sign a tab. This was a world of hitched rides and borrowed beds, and meals, if not scrounged, were desperately budgeted by appallingly hungry young men."

Punished by Rewards: The Trouble with Gold Stars,
Incentive Plans, A's, Praise, and Other Bribes
BY ALFIE KOHN

Former teacher Kohn throws down the gauntlet at society's blind acceptance of B. F. Skinner's "Do this and you'll get that" theory of behaviorism. This 1993 book ranges across school, work, and private life in its indictment of extrinsic motivators and paints a compelling picture of a world without them.

Type I Insight: "Do rewards motivate people? Absolutely. They motivate people to get rewards."

Kohn has written eleven books on parenting, education, and behavior—as well as scores of articles on that topic—all of which are interesting and provocative. There's more information on his website: www.alfiekohn.org.

Once a Runner
BY JOHN L. PARKER, JR.

Parker's novel, originally published in 1978 and kept alive by a devoted coterie of fans, offers a fascinating look into the psychology of distance running. Through the tale of college miler Quenton Cassidy, we see the toll that mastery can take—and the thrill it can produce when it's realized.

Type I Insight: "He ran not for crypto-religious reasons but to win races, to cover ground fast. Not only to be better than his fellows, but better than himself. To be faster by a tenth of a second, by an inch, by two feet or two yards, than he had been the week or year before. He sought to conquer the physical limitations placed on him by a three-dimensional world (and if Time is the fourth dimension, that too was his province). If he could conquer the weakness, the cowardice in himself, he would not worry about the rest; it would come."

The War of Art: Break Through the Blocks
and Win Your Inner Creative Battles
BY STEVEN PRESSFIELD

Pressfield's potent book is both a wise meditation on the obstacles that stand in the way of creative freedom and a spirited battle plan for overcoming the resistance that arises when we set out to do something great. If you're looking for a quick jolt on your journey toward mastery, this is it.

Type I Insight: "It may be that the human race is not ready for freedom. The air of liberty may be too rarified for us to breathe. Certainly I wouldn't be writing this book, on this subject, if living with freedom were easy. The paradox seems to be, as Socrates demonstrated long ago, that the truly free individual is free only to the extent of his own self-mastery. While those who will not govern themselves are condemned to find masters to govern over them."

Maverick: The Success Story Behind the
World's Most Unusual Workplace
BY RICARDO SEMLER

While many bosses are control freaks, Semler might be the first autonomy freak. He transformed the Brazilian manufacturing firm Semco through a series of radical steps. He canned most executives, eliminated job titles, let the company's three thousand employees set their own hours, gave everyone a vote in big decisions, and even let some workers determine their own salaries. The result: Under Semler's (non)command, Semco has grown 20 percent a year for the past two decades. This book, along with Semler's more recent *The Seven-Day Weekend*, shows how to put his iconoclastic and effective philosophy into action.

Type I Insight: "I want everyone at Semco to be self-sufficient. The company is organized—well, maybe that's not quite the right word for us—not to depend too much on any individual, especially me. I take it as a point of pride that twice on my return from long trips my office had been moved—and each time it got smaller."

The Fifth Discipline: The Art and Practice of the Learning Organization
BY PETER M. SENGE

In his management classic, Senge introduces readers to "learning organizations"—where autonomous thinking and shared visions for the future are not only encouraged, but are considered vital to the health of the organization. Senge's "five disciplines" offer a smart organizational companion to Type I behavior.

Type I Insight: "People with a high level of personal mastery are able to consistently realize the results that matter most deeply to them—in effect, they approach their life as an artist would approach a work of art. They do that by becoming committed to their own lifelong learning."

Listen to the Gurus:
Six Business Thinkers Who Get It

While the list of companies that embrace Type I thinking is distress-ingly short, the blueprints for building such organizations are readily available. The following six business thinkers offer some wise guid-ance for designing organizations that promote autonomy, mastery, and purpose.

DOUGLAS McGREGOR

Who: A social psychologist and one of the first professors at MIT's Sloan School of Management. His landmark 1960 book, *The Human Side of Enterprise*, gave the practice of management a badly needed shot of humanism.

Big Idea: Theory X vs. Theory Y. McGregor described two very different approaches to management, each based on a differ-ent assumption about human behavior. The first approach, which he called Theory X, assumed that people avoid effort, work only for money and security, and therefore need to be controlled. The second, which he called Theory Y, assumed that work is as natural for human beings as play or rest, that initiative and creativity are widespread, and that if people are committed to a goal, they will actually seek responsibility. Theory Y, he argued, was the more accurate—and ultimately more effective—approach.

Type I Insight: "Managers frequently complain to me about the fact that subordinates 'nowadays' won't take responsibility. I have been interested to note how often these same managers keep a constant surveillance over the day-to-day performance of subordinates, sometimes two or three levels below themselves."

More Info: As I explained in Chapter 3, *The Human Side of Enterprise* is a key ancestor of Motivation 3.0. Although McGregor wrote the book a full fifty years ago, his observations about the limits of control remain smart, fresh, and relevant.

PETER F. DRUCKER

Who: The most influential management thinker of the twentieth century. He wrote an astonishing forty-one books, influenced the thinking of two generations of CEOs, received a U.S. Presidential Medal of Freedom, and taught for three decades at the Claremont Graduate University Business School that now bears his name.

Big Idea: Self-management. "Drucker's primary contribution is not a single idea," Jim Collins once wrote, "but rather an entire body of work that has one gigantic advantage: nearly all of it is essentially right." Drucker coined the term "knowledge worker," foresaw the rise of the nonprofit sector, and was among the first to stress the primacy of the customer in business strategy. But although he's best known for his thoughts on managing businesses, toward the end of his career Drucker signaled the next frontier: *self-management*. With the rise of individual longevity and the decline of job security, he argued, individuals have to think hard about where their strengths lie, what they can contribute, and how they can improve their own performance. "The need to manage oneself," he wrote shortly before he died in 2005, is "creating a revolution in human affairs."

Type I Insight: "Demanding of knowledge workers that they define their own task and its results is necessary because knowledge workers must be autonomous . . . workers should be asked to think through their own work plans and then to submit them. *What am I going to focus on? What results can be expected for which I should be held accountable? By what deadline?*"

More Info: Drucker wrote many books, and many have been written about him, but a great starting place is *The Daily Drucker,* a small gem that provides 366 insights and "action points" for putting his ideas into practice. On the topic of self-management, read Drucker's 2005 *Harvard Business Review* article, "Managing Oneself." For more information and access to digital archives of his writing, check out www.druckerinstitute.com.

JIM COLLINS

Who: One of the most authoritative voices in business today and the author of *Built to Last* (with Jerry Porras), *Good to Great,* and, most recently, *How the Mighty Fall.* A former professor at the Stanford Graduate School of Business, he now operates his own management lab in Boulder, Colorado.

Big Idea: Self-motivation and greatness. "Expending energy trying to motivate people is largely a waste of time," Collins wrote in *Good to Great.* "If you have the right people on the bus, they will be self-motivated. The real question then becomes: *How do you manage in such a way as not to de-motivate people?*"

Type I Insight: Collins suggests four basic practices for creating a culture where self-motivation can flourish:

1.   "Lead with questions, not answers."
2.   "Engage in dialogue and debate, not coercion."
3.   "Conduct autopsies, without blame."
4.   "Build 'red flag' mechanisms." In other words, make it easy for employees and customers to speak up when they identify a problem.

More Info: Collins's website, www.jimcollins.com, contains more information about his work, as well as excellent diagnostic tools, guides, and videos.

CALI RESSLER AND JODY THOMPSON

Who: These two former human resources professionals at Best Buy persuaded their CEO to experiment with a radical new approach to organizing work. They wrote a book about their experiences, *Why Work Sucks and How to Fix It*, and now run their own consultancy.

Big Idea: The results-only work environment. ROWE, described in Chapter 4, affords employees complete autonomy over when, where, and how they do their work. The only thing that matters is results.

Type I Insight: Among the basic tenets of ROWE:

> "People at all levels stop doing any activity that is a waste
> of their time, the customer's time, or their company's
> time."
> "Employees have the freedom to work any way they want."
> "Every meeting is optional."
> "There are no work schedules."

More Info: You can learn more about ROWE at their website: www.culturerx.com.

GARY HAMEL

Who: "The world's leading expert on business strategy," according to *BusinessWeek*. He's the coauthor of the influential book *Competing for the Future*, a professor at the London Business School, and the director of the California-based MLab, where he's spearheading the pursuit of "moon shots for management"—a set of huge challenges to reform the theory and practice of running organizations.

Big Idea: Management is an outdated technology. Hamel likens management to the internal combustion engine—a technology that has largely stopped evolving. Put a 1960s-era CEO in a time machine and transport him to 2010, Hamel says, and that CEO "would find a great many of today's management rituals little changed from those that governed corporate life a generation or two ago." Small wonder, Hamel explains. "Most of the essential tools and techniques of modern management were invented by individuals born in the 19th century, not long after the end of the American Civil War." The solution? A radical overhaul of this aging technology.

Type I Insight: "The next time you're in a meeting and folks are discussing how to wring another increment of performance out of your workforce, you might ask: 'To what end, and to whose benefit, are our employees being asked to give of themselves? Have we committed ourselves to a purpose that is truly deserving of their initiative, imagination, and passion?'"

More Info: Hamel's *The Future of Management* (written with Bill Breen) is an important read. For more on Hamel's ideas and research, see www.garyhamel.com and www.managementlab.org.

The Type I Fitness Plan:
Four Tips for Getting (and Staying)
Motivated to Exercise

On the jacket of this book is a runner—and that's no accident. Running can have all the elements of Type I behavior. It's autonomous. It allows you to seek mastery. And the people who keep at it, and enjoy it most, often run toward a greater purpose—testing their limits or staying healthy and vital. To help you bring the spirit of intrinsic motivation out of the office and classroom and into another realm of your life, here are four tips for staying fit the Type I way.

Set your own goals. Don't accept some standardized, cookie-cutter exercise plan. Create one that's tailored to your needs and fitness level. (You can work with a professional on this, but you make the final calls.) Equally important, set the right kinds of goals. Ample research in behavioral science shows that people who seek to lose weight for extrinsic reasons—to slim down for a wedding or to look better at a class reunion—often reach their goals. And then they gain the weight back as soon as the target event ends. Meanwhile, people who pursue more intrinsic goals—to get fit in order to feel good or to stay healthy for their family—make slower progress at first, but achieve significantly better results in the long term.

Ditch the treadmill. Unless you really like treadmills, that is. If trudging to the gym feels like a dreary obligation, find a form of fitness you enjoy—that produces those intoxicating moments of flow. Gather some friends for an informal game of tennis or basketball, join an amateur league, go for walks at a local park, dance for a half-hour, or play with your kids. Use the Sawyer Effect to your advantage—and turn your work(out) into play.

Keep mastery in mind. Getting better at something provides a great source of renewable energy. So pick an activity in which you can improve over time. By continually increasing the difficulty of what you take on—think Goldilocks—and setting more audacious challenges for yourself as time passes, you can renew that energy and stay motivated.

Reward yourself the right way. If you're really struggling, consider a quick experiment with Stickk (www.stickk.com), a website in which you publicly commit to a goal and must hand over money—to a friend, a charity, or an "anti-charity"—if you fail to reach it. But in general, don't bribe yourself with "if-then" rewards—like "If I exercise four times this week, then I'll buy myself a new shirt." They can backfire. But the occasional "now that" reward? Not a problem. So if you've swum the distance you hoped to this week, there's no harm in treating yourself to a massage afterward. It won't hurt. And it might feel good.

Drive: The Recap

This book has covered a lot of ground—and you might not be able to instantly recall everything in it. So here you'll find three different summaries of Drive. *Think of it as your talking points, refresher course, or memory jogger.*

TWITTER SUMMARY*

Carrots & sticks are so last century. *Drive* says for 21st century work, we need to upgrade to autonomy, mastery & purpose.

COCKTAIL PARTY SUMMARY†

When it comes to motivation, there's a gap between what science knows and what business does. Our current business operating

---

*A maximum of 140 characters, as required by Twitter (see www.twitter.com). Feel free to retweet this summary or one of your own.

†A maximum of 100 words, or less than a minute of talking.

system—which is built around external, carrot-and-stick motivators—doesn't work and often does harm. We need an upgrade. And the science shows the way. This new approach has three essential elements: (1) *Autonomy*—the desire to direct our own lives; (2) *Mastery*—the urge to get better and better at something that matters; and (3) *Purpose*—the yearning to do what we do in the service of something larger than ourselves.

CHAPTER-BY-CHAPTER SUMMARY

Introduction: The Puzzling Puzzles of Harry Harlow and Edward Deci

Human beings have a biological drive that includes hunger, thirst, and sex. We also have another long-recognized drive: to respond to rewards and punishments in our environment. But in the middle of the twentieth century, a few scientists began discovering that humans also have a third drive—what some call "intrinsic motivation." For several decades, behavioral scientists have been figuring out the dynamics and explaining the power of our third drive. Alas, business hasn't caught up to this new understanding. If we want to strengthen our companies, elevate our lives, and improve the world, we need to close the gap between what science knows and what business does.

PART ONE. A NEW OPERATING SYSTEM

Chapter 1. The Rise and Fall of Motivation 2.0

Societies, like computers, have operating systems—a set of mostly invisible instructions and protocols on which everything runs. The first human operating system—call it Motivation 1.0—was all about survival. Its successor, Motivation 2.0, was built around external rewards and punishments. That worked fine for routine twentieth-century tasks. But in the twenty-first century, Motivation 2.0 is proving incompatible with how we organize what we do, how we think about what we do, and how we do what we do. We need an upgrade.

Chapter 2. Seven Reasons Carrots and Sticks (Often) Don't Work . . .

When carrots and sticks encounter our third drive, strange things begin to happen. Traditional "if-then" rewards can give us less of what we want: They can extinguish intrinsic motivation, diminish performance, crush creativity, and crowd out good behavior. They can also give us more of what we don't want: They can encourage unethical behavior, create addictions, and foster short-term thinking. These are the bugs in our current operating system.

Chapter 2a. . . . and the Special Circumstances When They Do

Carrots and sticks aren't all bad. They can be effective for rule-based routine tasks—because there's little intrinsic motivation to undermine and not much creativity to crush. And they can be more effective still if those giving such rewards offer a rationale for why the task is necessary, acknowledge that it's boring, and allow people autonomy over how they complete it. For nonroutine conceptual tasks, rewards are more perilous—particularly those of the "if-then" variety. But "now that" rewards—noncontingent rewards given after a task is complete—can sometimes be okay for more creative, right-brain work, especially if they provide useful information about performance.

Chapter 3. Type I and Type X

Motivation 2.0 depended on and fostered Type X behavior—behavior fueled more by extrinsic desires than intrinsic ones and concerned less with the inherent satisfaction of an activity and more with the external rewards to which an activity leads. Motivation 3.0, the upgrade that's necessary for the smooth functioning of twenty-first-century business, depends on and fosters Type I behavior. Type I behavior concerns itself less with the external rewards an activity brings and more with the inherent satisfaction of the activity itself. For professional success and personal fulfillment, we need to move ourselves and our colleagues from Type X to Type I. The good news is that

Type I's are made, not born—and Type I behavior leads to stronger performance, greater health, and higher overall well-being.

PART TWO. THE THREE ELEMENTS

Chapter 4. Autonomy

Our "default setting" is to be autonomous and self-directed. Unfortunately, circumstances—including outdated notions of "management"—often conspire to change that default setting and turn us from Type I to Type X. To encourage Type I behavior, and the high performance it enables, the first requirement is autonomy. People need autonomy over task (what they do), time (when they do it), team (who they do it with), and technique (how they do it). Companies that offer autonomy, sometimes in radical doses, are outperforming their competitors.

Chapter 5. Mastery

While Motivation 2.0 required compliance, Motivation 3.0 demands engagement. Only engagement can produce mastery—becoming better at something that matters. And the pursuit of mastery, an important but often dormant part of our third drive, has become essential to making one's way in the economy. Mastery begins with "flow"—optimal experiences when the challenges we face are exquisitely matched to our abilities. Smart workplaces therefore supplement day-to-day activities with "Goldilocks tasks"—not too hard and not too easy. But mastery also abides by three peculiar rules. Mastery is a mindset: It requires the capacity to see your abilities not as finite, but as infinitely improvable. Mastery is a pain: It demands effort, grit, and deliberate practice. And mastery is an asymptote: It's impossible to fully realize, which makes it simultaneously frustrating and alluring.

Chapter 6. Purpose

Humans, by their nature, seek purpose—a cause greater and more enduring than themselves. But traditional businesses have long considered purpose ornamental—a perfectly nice accessory, so long as it didn't get in the way of the important things. But that's changing—thanks in part to the rising tide of aging baby boomers reckoning with their own mortality. In Motivation 3.0, purpose maximization is taking its place alongside profit maximization as an aspiration and a guiding principle. Within organizations, this new "purpose motive" is expressing itself in three ways: in goals that use profit to reach purpose; in words that emphasize more than self-interest; and in policies that allow people to pursue purpose on their own terms. This move to accompany profit maximization with purpose maximization has the potential to rejuvenate our businesses and remake our world.

Drive: The Glossary

A new approach to motivation requires a new vocabulary for talking about it. Here's your official Drive *dictionary.*

Baseline rewards: Salary, contract payments, benefits, and a few perks that represent the floor for compensation. If someone's baseline rewards aren't adequate or equitable, her focus will be on the unfairness of her situation or the anxiety of her circumstance, making motivation of any sort extremely difficult.

FedEx Days: Created by the Australian software company Atlassian, these one-day bursts of autonomy allow employees to tackle any problem they want—and then show the results to the rest of the company at the end of twenty-four hours. Why the name? Because you have to deliver something overnight.

Goldilocks tasks: The sweet spot where tasks are neither too easy nor too hard. Essential to reaching the state of "flow" and to achieving mastery.

"If-then" rewards: Rewards offered as contingencies—as in, "If you do this, then you'll get that." For routine tasks, "if-then" rewards can sometimes be effective. For creative, conceptual tasks, they invariably do more harm than good.

Mastery asymptote: The knowledge that full mastery can never be realized, which is what makes its pursuit simultaneously alluring and frustrating.

Motivation 1.0, 2.0, and 3.0: The motivational operating systems, or sets of assumptions and protocols about how the world works and how humans behave, that run beneath our laws, economic arrangements, and business practices. Motivation 1.0 presumed that humans were biological creatures, struggling for survival. Motivation 2.0 presumed that humans also responded to rewards and punishments in their environment. Motivation 3.0, the upgrade we now need, presumes that humans also have a third drive—to learn, to create, and to better the world.

Nonroutine work: Creative, conceptual, right-brain work that can't be reduced to a set of rules. Today, if you're not doing this sort of work, you won't be doing what you're doing much longer.

"Now that" rewards: Rewards offered after a task has been completed—as in "Now that you've done such a great job, let's acknowledge the achievement." "Now that" rewards, while tricky, are less perilous for nonroutine tasks than "if-then" rewards.

Results-only work environment (ROWE): The brainchild of two American consultants, a ROWE is a workplace in which employees don't have schedules. They don't have to be in the office at a certain time or any time. They just have to get their work done.

Routine work: Work that can be reduced to a script, a spec sheet, a formula, or a set of instructions. External rewards can be effective in motivating routine tasks. But because such algorithmic, rule-based, left-brain work has become easier to send offshore and to automate, this type of work has become less valuable and less important in advanced economies.

Sawyer Effect: A weird behavioral alchemy inspired by the scene in *The Adventures of Tom Sawyer* in which Tom and friends white-wash Aunt Polly's fence. This effect has two aspects. The negative: Rewards can turn play into work. The positive: Focusing on mastery can turn work into play.

20 percent time: An initiative in place at a few companies in which employees can spend 20 percent of their time working on any project they choose.

Type I behavior: A way of thinking and an approach to life built around intrinsic, rather than extrinsic, motivators. It is powered by our innate need to direct our own lives, to learn and create new things, and to do better by ourselves and our world.

Type X behavior: Behavior that is fueled more by extrinsic desires than intrinsic ones and that concerns itself less with the inherent satisfaction of an activity and more with the external rewards to which that activity leads.

The *Drive* Discussion Guide:
Twenty Conversation Starters to
Keep You Thinking and Talking

These days authors might get the first word. But they don't—and shouldn't—get the last word. That's your job. So now that you've read this book, go out and laud or lash it on your blog or your favorite social networking site. But if you want to make the ideas in Drive *truly come to life, talk them over in person—with some colleagues from work, friends at school, or your book club. That's how the world changes—conversation by conversation. Here are twenty questions to get your conversation going.*

1. Has Pink persuaded you about the gap between what science knows and what organizations do? Do you agree that we need to upgrade our motivational operating system? Why or why not?

2. How has Motivation 2.0 affected your experiences at school, at work, or in family life? If Motivation 3.0 had been the prevailing ethic when you were young, how would your experiences have differed?

3. Do you consider yourself more Type I or Type X? Why? Think of three people in your life (whether at home, work, or school). Are they more Type I or Type X? What leads you to your conclusions?

4. Describe a time when you've seen one of the seven deadly flaws of carrots and sticks in action. What lessons might you and others learn from that experience? Have you seen instances when carrots and sticks have been effective?

5. How well is your current job meeting your need for "baseline rewards"—salary, benefits, a few perks? If it's falling short, what changes can you or your organization make?

6. Pink draws a distinction between "routine" work and "nonroutine" work. How much of your own work is routine? How much is nonroutine?

7. If you're a boss, how might you replace "if-then" rewards with a more autonomous environment and the occasional "now that" reward?

8. As you think about your own best work, what aspect of autonomy has been most important to you? Autonomy over what you do (task), when you do it (time), how you do it (technique), or with whom you do it (team)? Why? How much autonomy do you have at work right now? Is that enough?

9. Would initiatives like FedEx Days, 20 percent time, and ROWE work in your organization? Why or why not? What are one or two other ideas that would bring out more Type I behavior in your workplace?

10. Describe a time recently when you've experienced "flow." What were you doing? Where were you? How

might you tweak your current role to bring on more of these optimal experiences?

11. Is there anything you've ever wanted to master that you've avoided for reasons like "I'm too old" or "I'll never be good at that" or "It would be a waste of time"? What are the barriers to giving it a try? How can you remove those barriers?

12. Are you in a position to delegate any of the tasks that might be holding you back from more challenging pursuits? How might you hand off these tasks in a way that does not take away your colleagues' autonomy?

13. How would you redesign your office, your classroom, or your home—the physical environment, the processes, the rules—to promote greater engagement and mastery by everyone?

14. When tackling the routine tasks your job requires, what strategies can you come up with to trigger the positive side of the Sawyer Effect?

15. *Drive* talks a lot about purpose—both for organizations and individuals. Does your organization have a purpose? What is it? If your organization is for-profit, is purpose even a realistic goal given the competitive pressures in every industry?

16. Are you—in your paid work, family life, or volunteering—on a path toward purpose? What is that purpose?

17. Is education today too Type X—that is, does it put too great an emphasis on extrinsic rewards? If so, how should we reconfigure schools and classrooms? Is there an elegant way to reconcile intrinsic motivation and accountability?

18. If you're a mom or dad, does your home environment promote more Type I or Type X behavior in your child or children? How? What, if anything, should you do about it?

19. Does Pink underplay the importance of earning a living? Is his view of Motivation 3.0 a bit too utopian—that is, is Pink, if you'll pardon the pun, too rosy?

20. What are the things that truly motivate you? Now think about the last week. How many of those 168 hours were devoted to these things? Can you do better?

Your own questions:*

_____

_____

_____

_____

_____

_____

_____

*If you'd like your question included in the Discussion Guide for future editions of *Drive*, send it directly to me at dhp@danpink.com.

FIND OUT MORE—
ABOUT YOURSELF AND THIS TOPIC

Are you Type I or Type X?

Take the comprehensive, free online assessment at

www.danpink.com/drive.html

---

*Interested in regular updates on the science
and practice of human motivation?*

Subscribe to *Drive Times*, a free quarterly e-mail

newsletter at

www.danpink.com/drive.html

ACKNOWLEDGMENTS

And now a tip of the hat to those who kept me motivated.

At Riverhead Books, Jake Morrissey's skills as an editor were matched only by his talents as a therapist. He made this a better book without making its author a crazier person. Thanks also to Geoff Kloske, who threw his support behind this project early and enthusiastically—and to Riverhead's extraordinary production team for their skill and patience.

Rafe Sagalyn understood the promise of this book even before I did and championed it with his usual deft touch. I'm grateful to have him as a literary agent and a friend. A huge shout-out as well to the talented Bridget Wagner, who has spread the word about *Drive* to publishers around the world.

Vanessa Carr did a terrific job of finding obscure social psychology studies in the crevices of the Internet and on the dusty shelves of university libraries. Rob Ten Pas once again used his considerable talents to craft pictures to enliven my less considerable words. Sarah Rainone provided spectacular help pushing the project over the finish line during a hot and dreary summer. Remember all three of those names, folks. They're stars.

One of the joys of working on this book was having a few long conversations and interviews with Mike Csikszentmihalyi, Ed Deci, and Rich Ryan, who have long been heroes of mine. If there were any justice in the world, all three would win a Nobel Prize—and if that justice had a slight sense of humor, the prize would be in economics. Any errors or misinterpretations of their work are my fault, not theirs.

It's about at this point that authors who are parents apologize to their children for missed dinners. Not me. I don't miss meals. But I did skip nearly everything else for several months and that forced the amazing Pink kids—Sophia, Eliza, and Saul, to whom *Drive* is dedicated—into a dad-less existence for a while. Sorry, guys. Fortunately, as you've no doubt already discovered, I need you a lot more than you need me.

Then there's the threesome's mom, Jessica Anne Lerner. As always, Jessica was the first, last, and most honest sounding board for every idea I spit out. And as always, Jessica read every word I wrote—including many thousands of them aloud while I sat in a red chair cringing at their sound. For these small reasons, and many larger ones that are none of your business, this gorgeous, graceful woman leaves me slack-jawed—in awe and in love.

NOTES

INTRODUCTION: THE PUZZLING PUZZLES OF HARRY HARLOW AND EDWARD DECI

1. Harry F. Harlow, Margaret Kuenne Harlow, and Donald R. Meyer, "Learning Motivated by a Manipulation Drive," *Journal of Experimental Psychology* 40 (1950): 231.

2. Ibid., 233–34.

3. Harry F. Harlow, "Motivation as a Factor in the Acquisition of New Responses," in *Current Theory and Research on Motivation* (Lincoln: University of Nebraska Press, 1953), 46.

4. Harlow, in some ways, became part of the establishment. He won a National Science Medal and became president of the American Psychological Association. For more about Harlow's interesting life, see Deborah Blum, *Love at Goon Park: Harry Harlow and the Science of Affection* (Cambridge, Mass.: Perseus, 2002), and Jim Ottaviani and Dylan Meconis, *Wire Mothers: Harry Harlow and the Science of Love* (Ann Arbor, Mich.: G. T. Labs, 2007).

5. Edward L. Deci, "Effects of Externally Mediated Rewards on Intrinsic Motivation," *Journal of Personality and Social Psychology* 18 (1971): 114.

6. Edward L. Deci, "Intrinsic Motivation, Extrinsic Reinforcement, and Inequity," *Journal of Personality and Social Psychology* 22 (1972): 119–20.

Notes

CHAPTER 1. THE RISE AND FALL OF MOTIVATION 2.0

1. "Important Notice: MSN Encarta to Be Discontinued," Microsoft press release (March 30, 2009); Ina Fried, "Microsoft Closing the Book on Encarta," *CNET News*, March 30, 2009; "Microsoft to Shut Encarta as Free Sites Alter Market," *Wall Street Journal*, March 31, 2009. Up-to-date Wikipedia data are available at http://en.wikipedia.org/wiki/Wikipedia:About.

2. Karim R. Lakhani and Robert G. Wolf, "Why Hackers Do What They Do: Understanding Motivation and Effort in Free/Open Source Software Projects," in *Perspectives on Free and Open Software*, edited by J. Feller, B. Fitzgerald, S. Hissam, and K. Lakhani (Cambridge, Mass.: MIT Press, 2005), 3, 12.

3. Jurgen Blitzer, Wolfram Schrettl, and Philipp J. H. Schroeder, "Intrinsic Motivation in Open Source Software Development," *Journal of Comparative Economics* 35 (2007): 17, 4.

4. "Vermont Governor Expected to Sign Bill on Charity-Business Hybrid," *Chronicle of Philanthropy*, News Updates, April 21, 2008.

5. Muhammad Yunus, *Creating a World Without Poverty: Social Business and the Future of Capitalism* (New York: Public Affairs, 2007), 23; Aspen Institute, Fourth Sector Concept Paper (Fall 2008); "B Corporation," *MIT Sloan Management Review*, December 11, 2008, and http://www.bcorporation.net/declaration.

6. Stephanie Strom, "Businesses Try to Make Money and Save the World," *New York Times*, May 6, 2007.

7. Colin Camerer, "Behavioral Economics: Reunifying Psychology and Economics," *Proceedings of the National Academy of Sciences* 96 (September 1999): 10576.

8. Bruno S. Frey, *Not Just for the Money: An Economic Theory of Personal Motivation* (Brookfield, Vt.: Edward Elgar, 1997), 118–19, ix. See also Bruno S. Frey and Alois Stutzer, *Happiness and Economics: How the Economy and Institutions Affect Well-Being* (Princeton, N.J.: Princeton University Press, 2002).

9. Bradford C. Johnson, James M. Manyika, and Lareina A. Yee, "The Next Revolution in Interaction," *McKinsey Quarterly* 4 (2005): 25–26 .

10. Careful readers might remember that I wrote about this general topic in *A Whole New Mind: Why Right-Brainers Will Rule the Future* (New York: Riverhead Books, 2006). Look for it at your local library. It's not bad.

11. Teresa M. Amabile, *Creativity in Context* (Boulder, Colo.: Westview Press, 1996), 119. Amabile also says that, used properly and carefully, extrinsic motivators can be conducive to creativity—a point I'll examine more in Chapter 2.

12. Telework Trendlines 2009, data collected by the Dieringer Research Group, published by World atWork, February 2009.

Notes

CHAPTER 2. SEVEN REASONS CARROTS AND STICKS (OFTEN) DON'T WORK . . .

1. Mark Twain, *The Adventures of Tom Sawyer* (New York: Oxford University Press, 1998), 23.

2. Mark Lepper, David Greene, and Robert Nisbett, "Undermining Children's Intrinsic Interest with Extrinsic Rewards: A Test of the 'Overjustification' Hypothesis," *Journal of Personality and Social Psychology* 28, no. 1 (1973): 129–37.

3. Edward L. Deci, Richard M. Ryan, and Richard Koestner, "A Meta-Analytic Review of Experiments Examining the Effects of Extrinsic Rewards on Intrinsic Motivation," *Psychological Bulletin* 125, no. 6 (1999): 659.

4. Jonmarshall Reeve, *Understanding Motivation and Emotion*, 4th ed. (Hoboken, N.J.: John Wiley & Sons, 2005), 143.

5. Dan Ariely, Uri Gneezy, George Lowenstein, and Nina Mazar, "Large Stakes and Big Mistakes," *Federal Reserve Bank of Boston Working Paper No. 05-11*, July 23, 2005 (emphasis added). You can also find a very short summary of this and some other research in Dan Ariely, "What's the Value of a Big Bonus?" *New York Times*, November 20, 2008.

6. "LSE: When Performance-Related Pay Backfires," *Financial*, June 25, 2009.

7. Sam Glucksberg, "The Influence of Strength of Drive on Functional Fixedness and Perceptual Recognition," *Journal of Experimental Psychology* 63 (1962): 36–41. Glucksberg obtained similar results in his "Problem Solving: Response Competition Under the Influence of Drive," *Psychological Reports* 15 (1964).

8. Teresa M. Amabile, Elise Phillips, and Mary Ann Collins, "Person and Environment in Talent Development: The Case of Creativity," in *Talent Development: Proceedings from the 1993 Henry B. and Jocelyn Wallace National Research Symposium on Talent Development*, edited by Nicholas Colangelo, Susan G. Assouline, and DeAnn L. Ambroson (Dayton: Ohio Psychology Press, 1993), 273–74.

9. Jean Kathryn Carney, "Intrinsic Motivation and Artistic Success" (unpublished dissertation, 1986, University of Chicago); J. W. Getzels and Mihaly Csikszentmihalyi, *The Creative Vision: A Longitudinal Study of Problem-Finding in Art* (New York: Wiley, 1976).

10. Teresa M. Amabile, *Creativity in Context* (Boulder, Colo.: Westview Press, 1996), 119; James C. Kaufman and Robert J. Sternberg, eds., *The International Handbook of Creativity* (Cambridge, UK: Cambridge University Press, 2006), 18.

11. Richard Titmuss, *The Gift Relationship: From Human Blood to Social Policy,* edited by Ann Oakley and John Ashton, expanded and updated edition (New York: New Press, 1997).

12. Carl Mellström and Magnus Johannesson, "Crowding Out in Blood Donation: Was Titmuss Right?" *Journal of the European Economic Association* 6, no. 4 (June 2008): 845–63.

13. Other research has found that monetary incentives are especially counterproductive when the charitable act is public. See Dan Ariely, Anat Bracha, and Stephan Meier, "Doing Good or Doing Well? Image Motivation and Monetary Incentives in Behaving Prosocially," *Federal Reserve Bank of Boston Working Paper No. 07-9*, August 2007.

14. Bruno S. Frey, *Not Just for the Money: An Economic Theory of Personal Motivation* (Brookfield, Vt.: Edward Elgar, 1997), 84.

15. Nicola Lacetera and Mario Macias, "Motivating Altruism: A Field Study," *Institute for the Study of Labor Discussion Paper No. 3770*, October 28, 2008.

16. Lisa D. Ordonez, Maurice E. Schweitzer, Adam D. Galinsky, and Max H. Braverman, "Goals Gone Wild: The Systematic Side Effects of Over-Prescribing Goal Setting," *Harvard Business School Working Paper No. 09-083*, February 2009.

17. Peter Applebome, "When Grades Are Fixed in College-Entrance Derby," *New York Times*, March 7, 2009.

18. Uri Gneezy and Aldo Rustichini, "A Fine Is a Price," *Journal of Legal Studies* 29 (January 2000).

19. Gneezy and Rustichini, "A Fine Is a Price," 3, 7 (emphasis added).

20. Anton Suvorov, "Addiction to Rewards," presentation delivered at the European Winter Meeting of the Econometric Society, October 25, 2003. Mimeo (2003) available at http://www.cemfi.es/research/conferences/ewm/Anton/addict_new6.pdf.

21. Brian Knutson, Charles M. Adams, Grace W. Fong, and Daniel Hommer, "Anticipation of Increasing Monetary Reward Selectively Recruits Nucleus Accumbens," *Journal of Neuroscience* 21 (2001).

22. Camelia M. Kuhnen and Brian Knutson, "The Neural Basis of Financial Risk Taking," *Neuron* 47 (September 2005): 768.

23. Mei Cheng, K. R. Subramanyam, and Yuan Zhang, "Earnings Guidance and Managerial Myopia," *SSRN Working Paper No. 854515*, November 2005.

24. Lisa D. Ordonez, Maurice E. Schweitzer, Adam D. Galinsky, and Max H. Braverman, "Goals Gone Wild: The Systematic Side Effects of Over-Prescribing Goal Setting," *Harvard Business School Working Paper No. 09-083*, February 2009.

25. Roland Bénabou and Jean Tirole, "Intrinsic and Extrinsic Motivation," *Review of Economic Studies* 70 (2003).

Notes

CHAPTER 2A. . . . AND THE SPECIAL CIRCUMSTANCES WHEN THEY DO

1. Edward L. Deci, Richard Koestner, and Richard M. Ryan, "Extrinsic Rewards and Intrinsic Motivation in Education: Reconsidered Once Again," *Review of Educational Research* 71, no. 1 (Spring 2001): 14.
2. Dan Ariely, "What's the Value of a Big Bonus?" *New York Times*, November 20, 2008.
3. Teresa M. Amabile, *Creativity in Context* (Boulder, Colo.: Westview Press, 1996), 175.
4. Deci, Ryan, and Koestner, "Extrinsic Rewards and Intrinsic Motivation in Education."
5. Amabile, *Creativity in Context*, 117.
6. Deci, Ryan, and Koestner, "Extrinsic Rewards and Intrinsic Motivation in Education."
7. Amabile, *Creativity in Context*, 119.

CHAPTER 3. TYPE I AND TYPE X

1. Richard M. Ryan and Edward L. Deci, "Self-Determination Theory and the Facilitation of Intrinsic Motivation, Social Development, and Well-Being," *American Psychologist* 55 (January 2000): 68.
2. Meyer Friedman and Ray H. Rosenman, *Type A Behavior and Your Heart* (New York: Alfred A. Knopf, 1974), 4.
3. Ibid., 70.
4. Douglas McGregor, *The Human Side of Enterprise: 25th Anniversary Printing* (New York: McGraw-Hill, 1985), 33–34.
5. Ryan and Deci, "Self-Determination Theory and the Facilitation of Intrinsic Motivation, Social Development, and Well-Being."

CHAPTER 4. AUTONOMY

1. Edward L. Deci and Richard M. Ryan, "Facilitating Optimal Motivation and Psychological Well-Being Across Life's Domains," *Canadian Psychology* 49, no. 1 (February 2008): 14.
2. Valery Chirkov, Richard M. Ryan, Youngmee Kim, and Ulas Kaplan, "Differentiating Autonomy from Individualism and Independence: A Self-Determination Theory Perspective on Internalization of Cultural Orientations and Well-Being," *Journal of Personality and Social Psychology* 84 (January 2003); Joe Devine, Laura Camfield, and Ian Gough, "Autonomy or Dependence—or Both?: Perspectives from Bangladesh," *Journal of Happiness Studies* 9, no. 1 (January 2008).

Notes

3. Deci and Ryan, "Facilitating Optimal Motivation and Psychological Well-Being Across Life's Domains," citing many other studies.

4. Paul P. Baard, Edward L. Deci, and Richard M. Ryan, "Intrinsic Need Satisfaction: A Motivational Basis of Performance and Well-Being in Two Work Settings," *Journal of Applied Social Psychology* 34 (2004).

5. Francis Green, *Demanding Work: The Paradox of Job Quality in the Affluent Economy* (Princeton, N.J.: Princeton University Press, 2006).

6. "Atlassian's 20% Time Experiment," Atlassian Developer Blog, post by Mike Cannon-Brookes, March 10, 2008.

7. Quoted in *Harvard Business Essentials: Managing Creativity and Innovation* (Boston: Harvard Business School Press, 2003), 109.

8. The observation comes from former 3M executive Bill Coyne, quoted in Ben Casnocha, "Success on the Side," *The American: The Journal of the American Enterprise Institute*, April 2009. A nice account of 3M's practices appears in James C. Collins and Jerry L. Porras, *Built to Last: Successful Habits of Visionary Companies* (New York: HarperBusiness, 2004).

9. Erin Hayes, "Google's 20 Percent Factor," *ABC News*, May 12, 2008.

10. V. Dion Hayes, "What Nurses Want," *Washington Post*, September 13, 2008.

11. Martin Seligman, *Authentic Happiness: Using the New Positive Psychology to Realize Your Potential for Lasting Fulfillment* (New York: Free Press, 2004), 178; Paul R. Verkuil, Martin Seligman, and Terry Kang, "Countering Lawyer Unhappiness: Pessimism, Decision Latitude and the Zero-Sum Dilemma at Cardozo Law School," Public Research Paper No. 19, September 2000.

12. Kennon M. Sheldon and Lawrence S. Krieger, "Understanding the Negative Effects of Legal Education on Law Students: A Longitudinal Test of Self-Determination Theory," *Personality and Social Psychology Bulletin* 33 (June 2007).

13. William H. Rehnquist, *The Legal Profession Today*, 62 Ind. L.J. 151, 153 (1987).

14. Jonathan D. Glater, "Economy Pinches the Billable Hour at Law Firms," *New York Times*, January 19, 2009.

15. Cali Ressler and Jody Thompson, *Why Work Sucks and How to Fix It* (New York: Portfolio, 2008).

16. Tamara J. Erickson, "Task, Not Time: Profile of a Gen Y Job," *Harvard Business Review* (February 2008): 19.

17. Diane Brady and Jena McGregor, "Customer Service Champs," *BusinessWeek*, March 2, 2009.

18. Martha Frase-Blunt, "Call Centers Come Home," *HR Magazine* 52 (January 2007): 84; Ann Bednarz, "Call Centers Are Heading for Home," *Network World*, January 30, 2006.

Notes

19. Paul Restuccia, "What Will Jobs of the Future Be? Creativity, Self-Direction Valued," *Boston Herald*, February 12, 2007. Gary Hamel, *The Future of Management* (Boston: Harvard Business School Press, 2007).

20. Bharat Mediratta, as told to Julie Bick, "The Google Way: Give Engineers Room," *New York Times*, October 21, 2007.

21. See, for example, S. Parker, T. Wall, and P. Hackson, "That's Not My Job: Developing Flexible Employee Work Orientations," *Academy of Management Journal* 40 (1997): 899–929.

22. Marylene Gagné and Edward L. Deci, "Self-Determination Theory and Work Motivation," *Journal of Organizational Behavior* 26 (2005): 331–62.

CHAPTER 5. MASTERY

1. Jack Zenger, Joe Folkman, and Scott Edinger, "How Extraordinary Leaders Double Profits," *Chief Learning Officer*, July 2009.

2. Rik Kirkland, ed., *What Matters? Ten Questions That Will Shape Our Future* (McKinsey Management Institute, 2009), 80.

3. Mihalyi Csikszentmihalyi, *Beyond Boredom and Anxiety: Experiencing Flow in Work and Play*, 25th anniversary edition (San Francisco: Jossey-Bass, 2000), xix.

4. Ann March, "The Art of Work," *Fast Company*, August 2005.

5. This account comes from both an interview with Csikszentmihalyi, March 3, 2009, and from March, "The Art of Work."

6. Henry Sauerman and Wesley Cohen, "What Makes Them Tick? Employee Motives and Firm Innovation," *NBER Working Paper No. 14443*, October 2008.

7. Amy Wrzesniewski and Jane E. Dutton, "Crafting a Job: Revisioning Employees as Active Crafters of Their Work," *Academy of Management Review* 26 (2001): 181.

8. Carol S. Dweck, *Self-Theories: Their Role in Motivation, Personality, and Development* (Philadelphia: Psychology Press, 1999), 17.

9. Ibid.

10. Angela L. Duckworth, Christopher Peterson, Michael D. Matthews, and Dennis R. Kelly, "Grit: Perseverance and Passion for Long-Term Goals," *Journal of Personality and Social Psychology* 92 (January 2007): 1087.

11. K. Anders Ericsson, Ralf T. Krampe, and Clemens Tesch Romer, "The Role of Deliberate Practice in the Acquisition of Expert Performance," *Psychological Review* 100 (December 1992): 363.

12. For two excellent popular accounts of some of this research, see Geoff Colvin, *Talented Is Overrated: What Really Separates World-Class Performers from Everybody Else* (New York: Portfolio, 2008), and Malcolm Gladwell, *Outliers: The Story of Success*

(New York: Little, Brown, 2008). Both books are recommended in the Type I Toolkit.

13. Daniel F. Chambliss, "The Mundanity of Excellence: An Ethnographic Report on Stratification and Olympic Swimmers," *Sociological Theory* 7 (1989).

14. Duckworth et al., "Grit."

15. Dweck, *Self-Theories*, 41.

16. Clyde Haberman, "David Halberstam, 73, Reporter and Author, Dies," *New York Times*, April 24, 2007.

17. The passage is quoted in David Galenson, *Painting Outside the Lines: Patterns of Creativity in Modern Art* (Cambridge, Mass.: Harvard University Press, 2001), 53. See also Daniel H. Pink, "What Kind of Genius Are You?" *Wired* 14.07 (July 2006).

18. This study is explained in detail in Chapters 10 and 11 of Csikszentmihalyi's *Beyond Boredom and Anxiety*, which is the source of all quotations here.

19. Csikszentmihalyi, *Beyond Boredom and Anxiety*, 190.

CHAPTER 6. PURPOSE

1. United Nations Statistics Division, *Gender Info 2007*, Table 3a (2007). Available at http://www.devinfo.info/genderinfo/.

2. "Oldest Boomers Turn 60," U.S. Census Bureau Facts for Features, No. CB06-FFSE.01-2, January 3, 2006.

3. Gary Hamel, "Moon Shots for Management," *Harvard Business Review*, February 2009): p. 91.

4. Sylvia Hewlett, "The 'Me' Generation Gives Way to the 'We' Generation," *Financial Times*, June 19, 2009.

5. Marjorie Kelly, "Not Just for Profit," *strategy+business* 54 (Spring 2009): 5.

6. Kelly Holland, "Is It Time to Re-Train B-Schools?" *New York Times*, March 14, 2009; Katharine Mangan, "Survey Finds Widespread Cheating in M.B.A. Programs," *Chronicle of Higher Education*, September 19, 2006.

7. See the MBA Oath website, http://mbaoath.org/about/history.

8. Hamel, "Moon Shots for Management," p. 93.

9. Full disclosure: I worked for Reich for a few years in the early 1990s. You can read a short account of this idea at Robert B. Reich, "The 'Pronoun Test' for Success," *Washington Post*, July 28, 1993.

10. "Evaluating Your Business Ethics: A Harvard Professor Explains Why Good People Do Unethical Things," *Gallup Management Journal* (June 12, 2008). Available at http://gmj.gallup.com/content/107527/evaluating-your-business-ethics.aspx.

Notes

11. Elizabeth W. Dunn, Lara B. Ankin, and Michael I. Norton, "Spending Money on Others Promotes Happiness," *Science* 21 (March 2008).

12. Drake Bennett, "Happiness: A Buyer's Guide," *Boston Globe*, August 23, 2009.

13. Tait Shanafelt et al., "Career Fit and Burnout Among Academic Faculty," *Archives of Internal Medicine* 169, no. 10 (May 2009): 990–95.

14. Christopher P. Niemiec, Richard M. Ryan, and Edward L. Deci, "The Path Taken: Consequences of Attaining Intrinsic and Extrinsic Aspirations," *Journal of Research in Personality* 43 (2009): 291–306.

15. Ibid.

INDEX

Page numbers set in italics indicate illustrations.

Index

Index

Index

Index

Index

Index

Index